Achieve Personal Success in Enterprise IT Offshoring, Outsourcing and Captive Centre Management

By Clive Verrall

Copyright 2017 Clive Verrall

https://www.cliveverrall.com

This book is licensed for your personal enjoyment only. This book may not be re-sold or given away to other people. If you would like to share this book with another person, please purchase an additional copy for each person. If you're reading this book and did not purchase it, or it was not purchased for your use only, then please return to the website and purchase your own copy.
No part of this publication may be reproduced, distributed, or transmitted in any form or by any means, including photocopying, recording, or other electronic or mechanical methods, without the prior written permission of the author, except in the case of brief quotations embodied in critical reviews and certain other non-commercial uses permitted by copyright law. Thank you for respecting the hard work of this author.

~~~

Preface

This book will help you make a success of offshoring, outsourcing and managing captive centres. You may already be involved in offshoring today, your employer may have told you it is planning to offshore or you may have been asked to evaluate a company's strategy which includes offshoring. This book will help you from any of these starting points. You may have heard that offshoring saved one organisation millions of dollars but simultaneously another organisation is mysteriously reducing its outsourcing. But what does it really mean and are these subjects comparable? Reading this book will help you answer these questions for yourself and allow you to define and evaluate offshoring strategy.

Offshoring is a huge subject. It has its own vocabulary and its own set of specific skills which are not part of the mainstream. It has its own models and lifecycles. It is a product of the "flat world" and the interconnected global economy that we now live in. If you want to understand the practicalities of this subject in order to ensure your own personal success in offshoring, outsourcing, building an offshore centre, or in setting IT strategy or you are just curious about lifting the lid on this vast subject then this book will help you.

The book will focus on the offshoring of IT activities from corporate IT departments to their own offshore facilities or to an outsourcing vendor. It will also give examples of how this extends to cover non-IT Business Process Offshoring activities. This book includes advice and lessons learnt from real offshoring experiences. This is not a book about statistical trends in offshoring or untested management theory.

~~~

CONTENTS

1.	Onshore and Offshore	5
2.	Why offshore?	7
3.	Facing the Objections to Offshoring	12
4.	Eighteen Essential Offshoring Models	23
5.	Comparison of offshoring models	33
6.	How to source Captive Centre staff	61
7.	Recruiting permanent staff for the Captive Centre	75
8.	Why internal staff need redeployment	84
9.	Activity Full transition to offshore	86
10.	Are you ready for offshore managed services?	96
11.	How does the vendor make it work?	101
12.	Successful enterprise offshore planning	113
13.	Defining the Captive Centre strategy	123
14.	How to reduce Captive Centre long term costs	135
15.	Selecting and managing the vendors	141
16.	IT Offshoring Case Studies	156
Glossary		180
About the Author		185
Acknowledgements		186
Other books by this author		187

~~~

Onshore and Offshore

What do they mean?

To offshore an IT activity means to conduct some part of the IT activity outside the home country, typically in a developing country that provides cost advantages.

Onshore is where the IT activity originated from. It is the home location of the corporation.

There are three locations that you need to consider.
1. Onshore
2. Near shore
3. Offshore

Near shore can be understood to be an offshore location that is not far from the home location, therefore it is a local variant of offshoring. Throughout the book when I use the term offshore then I will be including near shore activities unless I make a specific exception and refer directly to near shore.

Onshore and Offshore in practice

In the IT context, onshore typically means a developed country with western world costs and offshore is the opposite, a developing country where costs remain below the general level of western costs for the foreseeable future. The offshore country is likely to be in a different continent to the onshore country.

The office in which the offshore (or near shore) work is conducted could be one of the following.

- A subsidiary of the parent company.
- An outsourcing vendor's office.
- A joint venture office.

There is no global register of which country is onshore and which offshore. In practice your organisation will have its own interpretation of which countries count as being offshore. An example of this could be Singapore, it is generally cheaper than the western world but not enough for all organisations to consider it as an offshore location.

Near shore is offshore too

If the advantages of long distance offshoring can be achieved without leaving the continent or the current time-zone then that location will be labelled near shore.

Choosing a near shore location over a faraway offshore location is typically a trade-off. For instance an organisation might be prepared to accept less cost savings in favour of being able to reach the location quickly to work on projects together or resolve problems.

Delocalising IT activities from onshore to near shore is still offshoring. The challenges, best practices, advantages and disadvantages that are presented in this book for offshoring apply equally to near shore activities. Near shore centres may also have the added attraction of offering languages that are not available in a global offshore centre.

An example of a near shore activity would be a company in Lille, France building an IT operations centre in Bucharest, Romania. Cost savings could be achieved but without the same risks associated with moving the activity far away to a global offshoring centre in India. A further advantage would be the ready availability of French language skills in Romania that would be more difficult to find in India. Despite this, the unit cost of staff in Romania may be higher than in India.

Note that near shore locations don't have to be in developing countries, but they do have to offer cost advantages compared to the home location.

~~~

Why offshore?

Cost reduction

The main objective of offshoring right from the very first days has been cost reduction. Without being able to promise a reduction in costs (however small) then no major offshoring activity would ever have started. Cost remains the biggest driver for offshoring.

Which costs can be reduced? The unit of cost to reduce could be the daily rate of an application tester, the total cost of supporting a global application, the cost of delivering a turn-key new application or cost reduction for the whole of the global IT department. It depends on the requirements and the engagement model that is chosen.

The most obvious cost reduction will be in the arbitrage of staff costs between countries, that is to say that staff will be cheaper in the offshore location. The use of best practices, process driven methods and technological strengths have also led to cost reductions compared to the IT department onshore.

Of course your target may not be in simply reducing costs, this could be an over simplification. You may be looking to make use of the lower offshore costs to deliver more IT services for the same money. In which case you are not aiming for a simple cost reduction. You want to use offshoring as a tool within a structured budget management plan to control the costs for the organisation as a whole.

Although cost reduction is the main objective, in recent years few organisations would offshore if they could only achieve cost reduction. They want more. This can be seen especially with the increase in near shoring, where cost reduction is less than can be achieved through long distance offshoring, but it is still increasing due to the added value that is being achieved. The next sections will explore the other advantages of offshoring that are attracting corporations.

Access to skilled IT resources

Once cost reduction has been established in principle it is common for organisations to have as their second offshoring goal to gain access to resources (the people who will do the IT work).

In the context of IT we regularly read in the press that there is an IT skills shortage. IT work simply can't go ahead if an organisation can't find enough people with the right skills. So the principle of cost saving is often not enough, an organisation wants to know that offshoring will also give access to the IT skills that match the current and future skills profiles. Many offshore locations have huge numbers of experienced IT resources.

Transformation synergies

If an organisation has a major programme of transformation to achieve a particular corporate goal then it might need offshoring to be part of that transformation. That is to say, the transformation project just wouldn't be viable unless some of the target activity takes place in a lower cost location. So in this case they need cost reduction but the true goal is the business transformation.

An example of this could be the goal to develop all new applications to work on mobile devices. The transformation programme may disband technology teams in high cost locations and create new mobile skilled teams offshore to achieve the business goal. However, without the offshoring cost savings this grand transformation may cost too much and would not get approval from senior management.

Another type of transformation synergy could be consolidating the number of IT suppliers (onshore and offshore) that an organisation uses today. The consolidation could be with one outsourcing vendor or one Captive Centre.

Access to better processes, methodologies and best practices

An organisation may know that its IT department doesn't have the skills needed to deliver something new or to do something differently.

By way of example, perhaps you want to develop a large application and you know that the processes and skills for doing this on-time and within budget are not within your organisation. Alternatively, perhaps you have never done structured application testing with test automation and now you need to. You may have evaluated that the time it would take to introduce these new ways of working onshore would be prohibitive.

For these reasons and more you may want to use the services of an outsourcing vendor (or a Captive Centre) to access their processes, methods and best practices. To engage the people in those organisations that already know how to use these tools and for them to deliver your new services.

Process standardisation

Conducting the analysis to consolidate activities offshore will highlight the differences that exist between the way work is conducted in different offices, in different countries or between different business lines within the same global corporation. Therefore consolidating these activities in one offshore centre becomes the catalyst to standardise the processes and tools being used.

This standardisation could lead to cost reduction, operational risk reduction and reduced time to add new activities.

Staff ramp-up and ramp-down

Perhaps your organisation can see ahead of them a year of increased IT staffing needs, but once that period is over then there will be no requirement for keeping these staff. You could locate these additional staff offshore. They could be supplied as part of an engagement with an outsourcing vendor or maybe within your own Captive Centre.
In the past the requirement to quickly increase staff numbers and then to reduce staff numbers was achieved through engaging contractors or consultants in your existing offices. With the offshoring of activities being more accessible than before, these staffing requirements could be met completely with offshore resources thus avoiding any pressure on seating in your existing premises.

Access to resources in another time zone

Your local application support staff may not cover all the time zones necessary for your users today. One solution would be to use staff in an offshore location to close the support gap. This could be achieved either because their normal working hours overlap with the required time zone or you ask them to work in shifts.

Similarly you may want to execute application tests during the night time in order for developers to be ready to fix any identified bugs when they come in the morning. This could be achieved by making use of offshore staff whose daytime overlaps with your night time.

Transfer of risk

An IT department can use managed services to transfer delivery risk or operational risk to a 3rd party organisation. An example would be to transfer the application production support for a suite of applications to an outsourcing supplier with the required production performance defined in a contractually binding SLA.

Before the transfer the IT department would have been at risk of adding more resources to the support activity to ensure that service levels were achieved (an additional cost), whereas after the transfer they have a fixed cost to pay and it is the outsourcing vendor's contractual responsibility to meet the SLA in whatever manner he wishes (e.g. additional resources, process improvement etc.).

Follow the client

Global service providers often have long term partnerships with their global clients. When the client expands its activities into a new part of the world then the service provider may set up a new office in that part of the world with the specific intention of ensuring that their client is well supported in their new endeavour.

Therefore when the client decides to offshore its activities, the global service provider may well follow them and create a new office in the offshore location from which it can provide the necessary services. This is most likely to be part of an agreed strategy with the client and not just an opportunistic move.

~~~

Facing the Objections to Offshoring

Are you convinced yet?

You may know a lot about offshoring already and be convinced that it works. Or you may have mixed feelings. Perhaps you can see how some easy things might work but you are not convinced that more complex examples could possibly work. Experienced outsourcing delivery managers will tell you that anything can work offshore and give you a long list of examples to prove it.

Typically I find that there are a number of objections that need to be overcome before you can reach your own conclusions.

Objection 1 - Lack of Experience

The most common objection I have heard is that transferring an activity from a team of people who have an average of 20 years of experience onshore to a team of people with an average of 5 years' experience offshore could never succeed. I have personally seen this scenario work many times and I will explain some of the reasons why.

Counting years of IT experience within the team is a poor yardstick to use as the only metric to decide if offshoring is possible or not.

Imagine this scenario. An onshore product team has an average of 20 years of experience each and they have done a great job of building the software product that now needs to be offshored. They take pride in having engineered such a master piece and regularly make improvements to it.

Are such in depth improvements really needed? Who is benefitting from it, the end users or the IT team? Shouldn't the product be in a maintenance phase by now?

The offshore team does have an average of 5 years of experience, although this is a pyramid structure so those at the bottom of the pyramid have 1 year of experience and one member at the top of the pyramid has 10 years of experience. All the members of the team have been trained well, they work in a team well together and are happy to accept that the more senior member knows more than they do. The junior member's work is systematically reviewed by a senior technical member. He provides all the architecture and design input. Each member of the team is dedicated to his career, none of them have much of a social life outside work and each is playing their part to get their family into the middle classes in their country. Above all they are motivated and hungry for success.

We should also consider processes and methodologies. It might be a relief to find that the offshore team is experienced in the particular agile methodology that the onshore manager believes is needed to make the project work. The methodology is relatively new, so no-one has 20 years of experience with this methodology but the offshore team can prove that it has delivered real projects using this approach.

The offshore organisation has a strong track record of making similar transitions of IT activity offshore. They know exactly what to ask for, what to document and how to teach their staff. This is their business and they are very good at it.

If you considered all these things, can you now imagine that the transition to this offshore team might work?

Objection 2 - Even we don't know how it works

Many people believe that a software product cannot be offshored if the current onshore team doesn't know about every feature and every line of code, or that the existing processes around the product are unstructured or that there is no up to date documentation. They cannot see how the knowledge can be transferred to the offshore team if it is not known to the current team.

Offshoring organisations will not be put-off by these issues but will be very specific on what the limits of their responsibilities will be. Perhaps they will increase the cost to the client of making this type of transition.

One extreme example to illustrate this would be a class of offshoring called "sunset" applications. Imagine that the client has a whole set of software applications that were developed long ago, in a technology that is now difficult to recruit for. The original team left long ago and the team has been completely rebuilt a number of times. The current team really don't know how every part of the application works and they have very little documentation. However, they continue to support the application in a limited way. The end client has no desire to expand the use of these legacy applications but they are business critical so they must continue to work.

The offshore organisation will offer a service where they will take this suite of applications and support them for the client. To do this they will use a very structured process to learn and document what they can from the client. Very quickly they will be able to do as much as the client can do.

Then they may go further to prevent future problems and start to reverse engineer the existing applications, producing designs and documentation like the client lost long ago. With this exercise complete the client maybe offered the option of replacing these applications with something more modern and maintainable. This would not have been possible without the investment first in offshoring and then in reverse engineering.

Part of the sunset agreement may be that functional improvements will not be allowed, or that only certain improvements to specific modules will be considered, or that the time frame for changes will be generously large. This helps make the offshoring engagement achievable until the applications reach the final sunset of their useful lives.

Objection 3 - They can't possibly know XYZ technology

If your organisation has implemented its own proprietary technologies then it is perfectly likely that an offshore organisation doesn't know that technology. But then if it is that proprietary then how do you hire new recruits for it today? If you have ever added new staff to this activity then you already have a training route of one kind or another and this can be repeated for the offshore team.

Perhaps you use an application testing suite that is not in the mainstream. Or you use a help desk system for IT production that is rarely used in this business sector. Expect an outsourcing vendor to either find people with the skills, or contact the supplier directly for training, or propose a plan where your onshore team will train the offshore staff.

Alternatively, if it is a new build and you insist that it has to be built with the latest XYZ technology and you know that having skills in this technology is rare, then you might well receive a pushback from the offshore organisation. They know that your senior management wants to have a business support tool for the right cost and afterwards it needs to be maintained. So, they might make a pitch to build the product you are after using technology that they already know and for which they can find people on the market. In return they will quote a much lower maintenance cost so the total cost of ownership will be reduced. It might not have been your vision of offshoring but it will be attractive to your senior management.

Remember that global technology companies have the same identical standards for technical certifications wherever you are in the world. If your requirement is to have a Microsoft MCSD Web Application certified developer in the team then that will be the same standard in Seattle or Egypt. Some staff in developing countries will even go so far as to take their certifications in a western country to avoid any doubt about the validity of their certificates.

Objection 4 – The team has to be close to the users

A particular IT product team may always have worked within seconds of being able to physically meet their users. It will be a new experience for them to work with people who are further away.

Of course this happens all the time, not just with offshoring. For instance, imagine that the end user activity expands and there are now users in two countries. How can the same IT team now be close to both user groups at the same time? Similarly, we have all seen companies who have cut costs by moving premises. They may leave the users in the prime real-estate corporate headquarters and move the IT teams out to the suburbs. The business doesn't fail because the resourceful IT team finds compensating strategies.

Instead of letting the users interrupt the IT team to talk about new functionality, organise a meeting with them once per week. Track all incidents and new functionality requests in a good tool and give the users access to it. If you don't have them already, you could create support email accounts, live chat services or create a support desk phone number that a member of the IT team anywhere in the world can answer. Use a quarterly e-survey to find out how the users feel about using the application and the support they have received.

Alternatively, you may believe that you need to be close to the users because you are using an agile methodology (e.g. Scrum or Extreme programming) where regular reviews with the user are needed. Many activities of this kind have succeeded offshore through the use of collaboration tools, especially screen sharing. If you try this and it doesn't work in your case then as the manager you will need to consider the business case of using a different way of working offshore. You may not have the luxury to continue extreme programming on the desk next to the user if the budget has been cut. The real mission is to deliver IT services within budget, not to promote one methodology or another.

There is no intention to deny the importance of having "face time" between the users and the IT team, but if costs must be reduced then discipline is needed to reduce the number of people in high cost locations. To this end the activity could be offshored but have someone physically meet with the onshore users for a few days every 3 months. Or in a large team, an onshore support person could be left next to the biggest user group.

Objection 5 – We don't speak the same language

Most offshoring staff speak English and most of their clients speak English. Therefore for most of the time communication will work well. Alternatively, it is possible that the client's first language is not English and the offshore team is more fluent in their local language than in English. If English is the only common language then they will still have to use it to communicate despite it not being their first language.

If an organisation has to make this work then it will need strategies to compensate for the lack of fluent English speakers, the heavily accented conversations and the possible misunderstandings. Many teams use instant messaging tools to supplement phone calls. With instant messaging it is possible to have an interactive discussion which is not possible by email. Educated people often have good written English language skills even if their spoken skills need more practice. There are other advantages as well, instant messaging is more permanent than a phone call and other members of the team can read what was discussed.

Video conferencing and video calls add non-verbal communication to the conversation (such as body language). This can also improve the quality of communication.

Above all, team decisions should be documented. Minutes of major meetings should be written and circulated. Specifications should be written down and test results published.

There may be a perceived cultural gap that could be an obstacle to communication. For example, the UK has a long history with India and therefore working with India seems quite natural. Germany does not have the same long history with India and therefore people may feel apprehensive. On the other hand, UK teams that are used to working with Indian staff offshore will feel the cultural difference when they work with Polish near-shore teams who tend to be more direct in their communication. In a professional world this should be a small obstacle to overcome in order to achieve the benefits of offshoring. The cultural gap can be reduced by spending time with offshore colleagues and organising cultural education for both teams.

I have often seen one team's ability to understand another increases as they work together. For example, you can get used to a heavy accent over time.

An alternative to using a global offshore centre where English is the common language, is to offshore your activities to a near shore centre where they have the language skills that you need. As an example, some Eastern European near shore vendors have staff that speak many European languages. Of course these near shore centres may not have all the technical skills of a global offshoring centre located in India or China.

Objection 6 – They don't have the business knowledge

You may have a lot of business knowledge in your team, but how much is really needed to offshore all or part of your IT activity? If a large amount of business knowledge is needed then the question must be asked if this is due to a lack of a defined process and a lack of documentation or is it something else.

Maybe today your team of programmers has a lot of business knowledge and it is unimaginable to find programmers with this amount of business knowledge offshore. Consider how the offshore team should be structured. There are Business Analysts offshore too. Maybe your offshore team should contain programmers and business analysts? Or maybe you could implement an extended team and keep some of your experts onshore, this could still lead to significant cost saving. A slightly more expensive option would be to second one of the onshore team members to the offshore location to work with the offshore team for a number of months or years until the necessary knowledge has been transferred.

Most activities in the IT department can be offshored even if a graduated 2 year transition is needed. However, there will always be applications developed directly by the users themselves (e.g. in Access or Excel) that the onshore IT department would be cautious to take responsibility for. The offshore organisation would have the same concerns.

Objection 7 – No defined process and no documents

You may have a team that delivers what the users need but you know that their approach is very ad-hoc. Maybe each developer in the team gets his instructions from different business end users and these requirements are not stored in a common repository. Each developer makes his changes, tests them himself, shows them to the user and adds them to the next release. Neither the changes nor the tests are documented. When that one developer is on holiday then no-one else in the team knows how to support those changes. Priorities are being managed by different business users and no single person knows what will be in the next release of the application.

This may seem like an exaggerated case to some of you, but to others you will remember that you have seen teams like this.

I concede that the activities of this team really couldn't be sent offshore or near shore without making improvements. The key question is whether the process improvements can be made by the onshore team before the transition, or whether the only way forward is to transfer the activity and fix the problems offshore. Whichever team makes the process improvements, they need to be done not just to achieve the offshoring but to reduce the enormous operational risks currently being faced.

With Agile processes in place then tools such as Wiki, Confluence or Rally can be used to capture the requirements expressed as stories. This will ensure that all requirements are captured and are available to all teams. The prioritisation of the analysis of these requirements and the subsequent development tasks can then be assigned within the team. A collaboration space, such as a Wiki or SharePoint, needs to be created to store designs and narratives on how the application works today and how it is supported. Then the application tests need to be stored in a centralised test repository tool. All these tools need to be accessible from onshore and offshore. With the tools in place the manager needs to assign clear roles to the team members and to document the process they will use to enhance and support the application. Finally the staff will need to be trained in the processes and tools.

Objection 8 – Not in that country

Maybe the offshoring destination has already been chosen and you have concerns about the choice. Unfortunately you can't address every problem but as a manager you can gather the facts and escalate them to your senior management for their attention. Be warned, if you do that then be prepared to offer solutions too.

Economic instability may lead to foreign exchange rate variations. Companies with global customers are used to selling products to different countries and being exposed to exchange rate risk. Maybe this is new for the IT department, but it needs to find out how the parent company manages this with clients and suppliers today. It may have a treasury department that hedges against these variations.

There could be concerns that the technical infrastructure in the chosen country is not as good as in the onshore location. This could well be true. The key question is whether the infrastructure is good enough to deliver the services that you need. What is the truth about the infrastructure? Do your competitors seem to manage in the same environment? How much network bandwidth is really needed? How can you compensate for electricity outages?

There may be a risk that the offshore office will not be available due to natural disasters (e.g. floods, earthquakes) or due to political risks (e.g. strikes). If you have a business continuity team then ask them to investigate. Ask the established players in that location how they manage these risks.

Objection 9 - It is not worth it anymore

Ever since I have been involved in offshoring, some people have been telling me that it is too late to get established offshore and that cost savings can no longer be achieved.

In a practical sense this has never proved to be true. I can only think of one example (that I know for sure) where an organisation closed its Captive Centre after a period of at least 10 years as the cost savings were no longer achievable. Even then, they didn't bring the activity back to the onshore location they moved it to another offshore location.

The geography of offshoring is directly linked to the economic growth of developing countries. The country that seems cheap today may not be so cheap in 10 years when you consider double digit wage growth.

However, the cost savings that can be achieved before the IT costs in the offshore location reach the costs of the onshore location may be so great that it is worth offshoring anyway. Also if this is a long period of time then there may be other reasons for offshoring that are strong enough for the organisation to continue to offshore to that location even when the cost savings diminish (e.g. skills availability).

~~

Eighteen Essential Offshoring Models

Why are there different models?

IT project work, IT operations, application testing and data management activities are complex subjects. Executing all or part of these activities in another country doesn't make them any simpler. To even propose offshoring, to evaluate the risks and estimate the cost savings a vocabulary is needed to define clearly how the offshore work will take place and how the people will interact with their colleagues in the onshore location (if at all).

The following models provide the building blocks needed to begin to understand and then evaluate an offshoring proposition.

Offshoring as Outsourcing

An outsourced offshore model is where a 3rd party organisation conducts the offshore activity on behalf of the client organisation. To do this the 3rd party uses its own staff who will work from its own offices. The 3rd party will no doubt express a preference for how the teams are managed, how the personnel are chosen etc. Although these are important they do not change the definition.

To simplify the vocabulary, Outsourced Offshoring is often shortened to Outsourcing.

In-house Offshoring

An in-house offshore model is the internal equivalent of outsourcing to an IT vendor. The IT team will be part of the same organisation as those requesting the work, although they will be in an office in an offshore location. In-house offshoring is an extension to the organisation's existing IT activities. Clearly the implication here is that the offshore team is managed by the parent organisation, although exactly which level of management needs to be clearly defined. Many different management models would still be classified as in-house offshoring.
Note that many globally focussed organisations with in-house offshore activities don't use the term offshore as they want their employees in the offshore location to feel that they are equal partners with their onshore colleagues. This is a noble intention but it is necessary to ensure that the local advantages and disadvantages that led the corporation to offshore in the first place are not ignored by treating everyone exactly the same.

Captive Centre

If you are employing the model of in-house offshoring then you need a secure space in which to conduct these activities. If this activity exists on an industrial scale then you will have a dedicated office building with local management and support staff. This combination of office, technical infrastructure, support services and staff is called a Captive Centre.

Typically a Captive Centre has no local business activities offshore as it only provides services to the global parent organisation onshore.

A true Captive Centre has the appearance of being in the parent company. Therefore it would be decorated inside in the manner of the parent company and more importantly it would have a trusted private network connection to the parent company computer network. As a result the IT infrastructure and services would be identical to the parent company. The offshore employees would access their applications and services, e.g. corporate email, from PCs built to the same parent corporate standard.

The Captive Centre must follow the core global procedures and principles of any other office of the parent company. This would include IT security rules, data protection and corporate compliance rules.
Because offshoring is a relatively new subject the terminology grows quite often. The following alternative names for a Captive Centre already exist: Internal ODC, a Wholly Owned Operating Subsidiary (WOOS), a Shared Services Centre (SSC) or a Global Insourcing Centre (GIC). In this book I will continue to use the term Captive Centre as it reduces the number of acronyms that need to be remembered and it avoids confusion with the vendor operated ODCs.

Vendor ODC

The alternative to an in-house Captive Centre is for a 3rd party to create and operate an Offshore Delivery Centre (ODC) on behalf of their client. Typically the physical office space is owned by the outsourcing vendor. All the staff are supplied by the outsourcing vendor and managed by their Human Resources function. The office would still be branded internally as if it was part of the client company. Even the physical security, such as the employee access cards, would still be operated as if it was the client's premises.

Depending on the outsourcing vendor and the contract that is signed, the outsourcing vendor may also offer services to the ODC over and above what is achieved by the headcount that is seated in the ODC. For example, I have witnessed outsourcing vendors including their non-ODC expert staff in the project lifecycle process to achieve design reviews. This was an advantage as it added a level of industrialisation that the client did not have at that time.

Alternatively, if the outsourcing vendor's ODC is not a separate physical office then it maybe a Virtual ODC. This is simply the creation of multiple Vendor ODCs for different clients by subdividing a larger office of the outsourcing vendor. For example, the outsourcing vendor may have one big building with perhaps 20 separate client virtual ODCs. The advantage of this model is that the ODC can be established quickly (no additional office space needs to be leased) and it is possible to ramp up or ramp down the size of the ODC by moving the internal walls.

Offshore Partner

In terms of models, an offshore partner is an outsourcing vendor with whom you plan to have a long term relationship. This could mean that a contract, stating a guaranteed minimum amount of work, has been signed with the outsourcing provider. The typical length would be around 5 years.

The advantage is that the vendor will aim to keep enough staff in place that the offshore team begins to integrate with the client organisation. One of the attractive goals is that business knowledge and internal knowledge about the client's systems is retained and not lost in the way it would be if you were to change outsourcing vendors on a regular basis.

For the purposes of the analysis in this book, offshore partners will be considered as outsourcing vendors. The difference in the length of contract signed will not make any material difference to the comparisons or advice given in this book.

Build Operate and Transfer (BOT)

If an organisation has a preference for in-house offshoring but doesn't have the resource availability to do it then it may enter into a Build Operate and Transfer (BOT) agreement with an outsourcing vendor.

Effectively they contract with an outsourcing vendor to build an ODC and then to operate it for a fixed number of years. After which they would then transfer ownership to the client organisation. At this stage it would become a Captive Centre.

Clearly this would be unlikely to start life as a virtual ODC as the target would be to have a physical office that is owned by the client organisation and would have no further links to the outsourcing vendor.

Body Shopping and Staff Augmentation

In many organisations the first step that they take towards any type of offshoring is to start with body shopping. In this model an outsourcing vendor supplies staff from their offshore location to work on-site at the client's onshore location. The staff would act as contract or temporary staff and would work under the direct management of the onshore teams. This is an alternative to engaging contractors in the onshore market.

This may solve an initial resource availability problem but it is not a scalable solution. However, it can help to build trust that people from the offshore location have the necessary skills and that the onshore organisation may want to work with that outsourcing vendor.

Of course if an organisation is only doing body shopping in this way then it cannot claim that it is offshoring. For it to be offshoring it must have staff out of the country in an offshore location, not just employing staff that come from an offshore location.

The next type of body shopping takes place when a captive centre has been established and it is short of permanent staff. In this situation the captive centre may choose to engage staff from an outsourcing vendor in a body shopping mode. Again this may also lead to increased trust with the outsourcing vendor and hence more outsourcing vendor staff being engaged.

Many outsourcing companies don't advertise that they body shop their staff to their clients as it is a low value add business model for them. They can make more money selling services. As a result these outsourcing vendors tend to refer to body shopping as staff augmentation which makes it sound more like a service.

Extended teams

Often the first step into real offshoring is to establish an extended team. An onshore IT team recruits additional team members in an offshore location. They remain under the management of the onshore team manager and work together as one team. The motivation could be to expand the team in order to do more work but at a reduced cost compared to recruiting the additional staff onshore, or it could be to achieve a cost reduction by transferring roles from onshore to offshore.

The newly created offshore team does not have complete autonomy. The onshore manager has simply extended his team to the offshore location and he will directly manage each member of the offshore team in the same way that he manages his onshore team.

Managed services

In contrast to the extended team, a managed service is said to be provided from the offshore location when the offshore team is autonomous and its success is measured by its deliveries.

Therefore the offshore team will have autonomy in planning work, allocating tasks to the team members, recruiting new staff and executing its own work. The managed service team will receive high level work requests such as "build this application", or "add this feature" or "resolve this incident". They will have to make sense of these requests from the level of detail provided or through further questioning with the requestor. There will not be any additional IT staff to intermediate.

The success of the managed service team will be determined purely from the quality of their deliveries, the promptness of deliveries and the cost of the service. These attributes may be defined in a Service Level Agreement that is then used by the onshore organisation to manage the offshore team.

Follow the sun

If an organisation has offices around the world then it is possible to transfer responsibility for IT work from office to office throughout the day in order to provide a 24 hour service that "follows the sun".

Typically this requires three offices: one in Asia, one in Europe and one in America. The work day starts in Asia and then rotates with staff handing over the responsibility of their work at the end of the local working day. Most often this model is used for Application Production Support where support tasks are short in duration and therefore few tasks are handed over. The next location simply picks up the next task that has not been started. More recently this idea has been extended to software testing and even software development. The key to making this work is how to achieve a successful handover between teams at the end of the local working day.

Centralisation

An alternative approach to providing a 24 hour service is to centralise it. One team in one location does all the work. Typically this is achieved by splitting the working day into three shifts so that some staff work in the early morning, others in the afternoon and the third group work at night. Despite being in the same location, the need for a high quality hand-over still exists because the staff change with each shift.

Shared Utilities

A shared utility may be created as the result of a major transformation project. Often the cost savings achieved from offshoring underpins the business case for the transformation.

In a shared utility service, similar activities are bundled together to achieve economies of scale. This can be as simple as identifying all the teams that support product X, combining the support for product X into one team and then offshoring this support. Or it could require migrating users of product Y to product X within the same team and then offshoring this team. This requires a high level of industrialisation.

Full service offshoring

Many organisations will start by offshoring one type of activity, for example that could be application production support. In the end, greater efficiency may be achieved by offshoring the complete IT activity for a whole product or business line offshore. This will result in moving: design, development, testing, and application production support offshore. These teams would then be collocated so that they can work together and improve their efficiency.

This idea can be extended beyond IT activities. I have personally been involved in offshoring business operations teams and collocating them with the IT teams that built, supported and tested their applications. Everyone benefitted from the improved communication and increased team spirit.

Product oriented offshoring or technology oriented offshoring

A large Captive Centre has two choices on how to organise its teams: by product or by technology. Typically the organisation will have grown around a product, so teams will have become specialists in one software product or another. They will have gained some business knowledge and will have been able to apply that to their understanding of the software. The technical skills of each team will need to mirror the technologies used in their product. There is an alternative where teams are organised around technologies. For example all the software products written in JAVA will be under the same IT manager and he will allocate his JAVA resources to the product related tasks as necessary.

Lift and Shift or Fix and Shift

Many people are convinced that their activity could be offshored if only the current problems it is facing could be cured first. In the terminology of offshore transformations this is referred to as "Fix and Shift". An investment needs to take place to resolve the problems before the activity can be shifted and transitioned to offshore.

The alternative taken by many outsourcing vendors and mature offshoring organisations is to "Lift and Shift". In this model they don't wait for the onshore team to solve the problems they simply transfer the activity offshore and build time and resources into the offshore transition plan to fix the problems from the offshore location.

Fixed Price Engagement or Time and Materials

If it is a time and materials engagement then the number of days worked and the expenses incurred will be used to calculate the total cost. Therefore the quote received from the vendor may only have been an estimate of the total costs and will not match the final invoice.

Alternatively, if it was a fixed price engagement with the vendor then they are contractually obliged to only invoice the client for the cost agreed in the contract.

~~~

Comparison of offshoring models

Practical Analysis

The purpose of this book is to be practical about offshoring not purely theoretical. This section takes the concepts of the models that were just introduced and advises what the real differences are in order to expose their suitability to real world situations. At the end of each section you will be asked to imagine two different scenarios, the outcome of each one favours a different choice of model.

The following criteria are used in each comparison where relevant.

- Time to kick-off
- Scale up expansion
- Staff turnover risk
- Complex transition
- Simple transition
- Further savings
- Onshore skills
- Adding new skills
- Cost

I have had to make many generalisations and you will be able to find lots of exceptions in real life. However, the intention is to show you how it can work and to be practical.

Outsourced Offshoring versus In-house Offshoring

Let's assume in this analysis that the outsourcing vendor is a tier-1 major player with years of experience and that the in-house offshoring is for a major corporation.

Following a signed agreement, the time taken for the initial team to be deployed will appear to be very fast for the outsourcing vendor compared to the captive centre. The main reason for this is that this is the outsourcing vendor's business, he has done this many times and he is very good at it. He will have a pool of staff waiting to be deployed to projects that are immediately available and he will have the power to pull a limited number of people from existing client projects into the new project if his management agree that this makes commercial sense. The in-house team will probably be reliant on recruiting staff on the open market because their managers will be less open to releasing their key players from existing teams. In addition the in-house team is likely to have very high and specific standards on the people they want to recruit. So the build-up of the initial internal team will seem slow.

Similarly the outsourcing vendor will be at an advantage when it comes to scaling up the initial team. Beyond the advantages already stated, he will have an attractive brand for IT staff to want to join the organisation and a very well-oiled machine for both graduate recruitment and more mature hires. In comparison, the in-house offshore team is likely to continue to recruit high quality staff, all be it more slowly due to its internal constraints.

Next look at the vendor staff turnover from the client's perspective. This will have the appearance of being a lot higher than the average attrition figures that the outsourcing vendor shows the client. The client is interested in the rate of vendor staff departures on his own IT activities and much less interested by the official attrition rates of the vendor spread out across all their clients.

The outsourcing vendor will make all sorts of promises to leave the client with the dream team that he first proposed but for one reason or another staff will move. Remember that the outsourcing vendor has probably trained these staff from fresh graduates and if a staff member is getting restless then he would rather move them to another client's activity than risk losing them.

With awareness of this problem, the in-house team should have recruited people that accept that they need to stay on one particular product area and earn their stripes. This should lead to less attrition. The downside of this is that the Captive Centre will probably have less opportunities to offer the staff member when he does become restless. Therefore without forward planning and flexibility the person will eventually leave.

The quality of the transition to offshore is key because if the offshore team can't take on the work of the onshore team then no cost savings will have been made, or worse the productive capacity of the whole team will have been compromised. I have seen many teams that have accepted offshoring because it was dictated by their boss but in practice they continued doing the work of the offshore team as well as their own work. Clearly a frustrating waste of everyone's time.

You will not find better skills for transitioning an activity offshore than those of a sophisticated tier-1 outsourcing vendor. They will have well tried, tested and documented procedures for transition that their staff have been trained on. Despite this their model is intended for transfer as fast as possible which has its limitations. Also take in to account that the on-shore team that is about to lose their jobs will have limited willingness to share information with the outsourcing vendor. Also the outsourcing vendor would benefit greatly from the client having a strong product development process with lots of documentation, unfortunately this is something that lots of end user IT departments don't have.

The onshore team may well be unstructured but they will have inducted many new members into their team over the years and as a result will have practical experience of how to expose new joiners to more complex tasks as they climb the team ladder. Also the onshore team is likely to be more welcoming of an offshore resource when it is explained to them that he works for the same global organisation that they do and that they need to help each other.

Simple products can be transitioned offshore very quickly using the outsourcing vendor's structured approach. But for all the reasons I have just explained, there is a high risk in quickly transitioning an unstructured product that requires lots of business knowledge. The in-house process is typically a lot slower but more successful over the long term for these types of products.

The outsourcing vendor will have seen many offshore transitions and will be well placed to use his experience to propose long term improvements to the client's product or processes that the client would not have thought of or would not have wanted to take the risk of doing. These ideas could be quite radical. For example, a proposal to merge two products together and save money on support or re-write a product completely in another technology and save on maintenance costs. So with the outsourcing vendor's experience he is more likely to propose radical long term improvements. In fact, in a managed service proposal it is quite common for the outsourcing vendor to propose a reduction of staff (and or costs) after a year or two. Often this is not related to any scientific analysis but simply that the outsourcing vendor is convinced that the client never needed so many people in the first place.

The biggest difference for onshore senior management between these two models is the need to manage the outsourcing vendor. The client will need to be very accomplished at vendor management to make a success of vendor outsourcing. IT departments that are unstructured, poorly documented, person dependant and highly trusting of people will struggle. On the other hand, internal IT departments that are used to subcontracting IT activities to on-shore providers will probably find the transition to vendor outsourcing quite natural.

The vendor will find it much easier to add staff with new skills if necessary, especially if they are already available within his organisation. Adding these same skills to the in-house team will probably require recruitment.

In my experience the cost of paying an outsourcing vendor to provide an IT service with his staff from his premises is very similar to the cost of providing the same service from your own captive centre. Unfortunately, the cost tends to increase if you ask the outsourcing vendor to put his staff or his teams into your office. The outsourcing vendor will charge you a similar cost to having the staff in his own premises but when you add on the cost of providing those extra desks in your premises then the total cost will have increased.

Having asked for an explanation on why no discount is received from the staff not being in the outsourcing vendor's premises I have been told that their premises overheads are extremely low. Personally, I think it is just as likely that they want to make the option of working in their premises more attractive because it suits their business model.

Scenario example 1.
Imagine a corporation based in the United States that has been used to subcontracting IT projects and infrastructure support to a number of service providers in the US. If their local subcontracting had been very successful then as a result their IT department might already be lean in size. They might be looking for further cost savings, to reduce the number of companies that they are working with and to gain access to new technology and skills that are in high demand in their home country. A good solution for them could be to outsource their subcontracted IT work to India.

Scenario example 2.
Alternatively, imagine a conservative corporation in the United States with a strong culture that has never subcontracted IT work and has kept everything in-house. They may see their IT as a competitive advantage for the market that they are in. They couldn't imagine working with third parties and as a result they have little experience of managing vendors. Their HR organisation is strong and they are used to recruiting and supporting IT teams. However, their IT department is large and they are unable to sustain this many headcount in a high cost location. They are looking for a solution. For this corporation it maybe more natural to take the path of in-house offshoring and to open a Captive Centre in India. They could build a captive in their own image and hire staff that fit into their culture. Staff from the captive centre could spend long periods with their colleagues in the United States until the captive staff are really integrated with the parent company. Cost can be saved by slowly releasing staff in the home location.

Vendor ODC versus Captive Centre

In this comparison consider the establishment of an offshore centre, the management team and the additional support services not the recruitment of the frontline IT staff.

The outsourcing vendor is likely to be ready to create his ODC with management and support staff very quickly, especially if it is a virtual ODC. Despite this, the outsourcing vendor ODC is of no operational use until it is connected to the network of the client company and the outsourcing vendor staff are issued with appropriate client company specific PCs and other communication devices. In my experience, when the physical office building already exists, the network connectivity lead time has taken as long as 6 months. The longest lead time being to get approval from the global client organisation that a connection can be made and then completing the leased line connectivity. This requires form filling, security reviews, meeting with network architects, waiting for official decisions and the time taken for the physical network connection.

One could imagine that in an organisation that is used to giving vendors access to their network, perhaps through regularly subcontracting IT projects, that they would be a lot quicker in implementing the network connections.

If the management team or support staff in the offshore centre needed to scale up then the outsourcing vendor would be much quicker than the Captive Centre for exactly the same reasons as those for the front line IT staff stated in the previous section. The outsourcing vendor is very good at sourcing staff but the Captive Centre quality control is likely to be higher.

Turnover among the management and support staff of the outsourcing vendor ODC is likely to be higher than the Captive Centre. Despite this, as long as the transitions are managed, it is only the turnover amongst the front-line management staff that is likely to be noticeable or impacting to the client. Also the more mature management staff would have a lower turnover than the younger front line IT staff that interact with the client.

The outsourcing vendor will do everything he can to bring the culture of the vendor ODC as close as possible to the Captive Centre, but he will not reach the same level of integration. The staff in the Captive Centre will really believe they are part of the parent organisation and will be treated as such by the onshore teams.

There could be limitations in which activities can be offshored to the outsourcing vendor ODC. I have come across situations where offshore access to client personal data was agreed with the regulator in the client's country with the stipulation that the data must remain within the organisation and cannot be subcontracted in any way. This is something that you would need to find out for your own business.

Security can be good in both the vendor ODC and in the in-house Captive Centre but with different strengths. The vendor will aim to achieve high security through processes and procedures. For example, the vendor knows that he cannot afford to let someone steal credit card personal data so he makes every employee deposit his personal belongings in a locker before entering the ODC, this even includes barring mobile phones. In contrast, the Captive Centre follows the exact security procedures of the parent company and therefore knows it is achieving the same level of security. Despite this, the vendor always has the risk that he is sharing something that could cause data leakage. For example, the vendor ODC is shared with other clients or the network connection from the client could be made available to non-authorised people by accident. The Captive Centre is dedicated to the parent company and is physically isolated from everyone else, the vendor ODC has the risk of not being isolated.

Scenario example 1.
Imagine a European corporation that wants to enter a new market and as a result has a need to build a major new client facing application. They have some funds for this business expansion but they don't yet have the staff. The business management are pushing hard to deliver the new application as fast as possible. The corporation knows that if it builds the application in Europe then it will take time to recruit a new team and they don't believe that their HR department has the capacity either. The application is to last for some years to come and therefore needs to be in the latest technologies, hiring people with these skills will be even more difficult. They have considered subcontracting to a third party but this application will be critical to their new business and they don't like the idea of giving so much knowledge and control to a third party. Instead, they choose to create an ODC with an outsourcing vendor in China. This would allow them to have the staff they need very quickly and without having to do the recruitment themselves. The ODC will ensure they have their own team which are dedicated to their projects, including the future maintenance of this new application, and who will retain the knowledge of their applications and business practices.

Scenario example 2.
Alternatively, imagine a European banking organisation that also wants to enter into a new market. As they are a bank they have a strong culture of client data confidentiality in addition to their regulatory requirements. The new market will require a new application for which they are not in a position to recruit locally. When the application is live then it will also need to be supported, this will mean that IT production staff will be able to see certain confidential client details. This work has to take place offshore as it would be too expensive onshore and they don't believe they will find enough staff with the right skills in their home location. The IT department can see that they have two good solutions: one would be to ask a vendor to create an ODC for them, the other would be to open a Captive Centre. Their need to work with an offshore team who share their IT culture is critical to them, they can also see that it will be easier to convince the market regulators that they are doing everything they can for client confidentiality if they keep the activity in-house. Therefore they choose to create their own Captive Centre for IT development and production support.

Joint Venture, BOT or just BO?

Many organisations want a successful outsourcing vendors' help in setting up their offshore activity. To do this they may create a new joint venture company with the vendor. Typically the outsourcing vendor brings the offshore IT expertise and the key staff, while the client helps with the investment costs.

To all practical intents and purposes the joint venture company will create an ODC very much like an outsourcing vendor ODC except that the initial investment could be reflected in lower monthly bills to the client. The ODC may be branded like one of the client's offices but it would follow the procedures, methodologies and best practices of the vendor. This is because the client really wants to benefit from using the vendor's expertise to build the offshore centre rather than extending its own IT department.

The creation of an ODC, with or without a joint venture, could well be stated in a Build Operate and Transfer contract. This gets its name from the BOT model used for huge physical construction projects such as bridges and toll roads. The aim is to use the vendor's expertise to build the facility (e.g. bridge or ODC) and then to completely transfer the working product to the ownership of the client. An IT ODC is likely to be transferred after 2 full years of operation or later if the client chooses to defer it.

This model has been used successfully in construction projects for decades. However, in practice for IT ODCs we hear that fairly often the "transfer" phase never takes place. So in these cases an ODC is built, but the outsourcing vendor continues to run the activity because the client never exercises his right to start the transfer.

There may be many reasons for this. Some outsourcing vendors have told me in private that because the client never built the ODC that they have never had hands on experience of managing IT teams in that part of the world, for example they don't know how to manage attrition. When they realise this then they know that they are not ready to take over. Another theory is that if the vendor is making it work, why change it. Also some clients fear that the vendor will start moving key staff back to the parent company before the ownership transfer and therefore they will end up with a diluted management team.

The main advantage of entering into a joint venture is to give the client control over the offshoring asset that they have a share in. Using this control they can make sure that the services rendered by the ODC are for their benefit. If the client had created a Joint Venture with the outsourcing vendor then by the time the ODC has been operational for a few years they may have seen their investment appreciate. They could then sell their stake back to the vendor (and perhaps continue to use the vendors services) or sell to a third party.

Scenario example 1.
Imagine a new company in the west that needs to build many IT applications for internal and client use. The new company doesn't have an IT department but it knows that IT is an important enabler of its strategy. In the beginning the company prefers a strategy that allows it to focus on making a success of the new business and it sees building an IT department at this time as a distraction. In their long term strategy they know that the quality of their IT applications is key and that they will need to be in control of this. They choose to enter into a BOT with a major outsourcing vendor. This allows them to delegate as much as possible to the vendor at the beginning when they are focusing on their new business and it gives them the option to take control of the ODC in the years to come when their focus will have changed. When the time comes to transfer ownership of the ODC an appraisal of the situation can be taken and the company can defer the transfer of control if it is still not ready.

Extended Team versus Offshore Managed Service

This comparison looks at two ways to manage teams within a Captive Centre and the way in which these teams interact with their colleagues onshore.

If the intention is to create a managed service team then it must have a high degree of autonomy. There must be a local manager who can break the work packages into tasks, share them amongst the team members and manage the completion of their tasks to achieve the whole package. Therefore the quantum of work instructed is large.

The extended team is like having extra people in the onshore team who just happen to be sat further away and who make use of technology to compensate for being in a different location. In the extended team they will not be expected to break the work into tasks as that is the responsibility of their team manager in the onshore location. They will receive tasks directly from him.

The accountability of the managed service team is very high. It is highly visible if they don't deliver the large pieces of work that they are asked to do. Conversely, it is possible that the extended team can deliver poor quality work or no work at all and the onshore team can compensate for them.

In the beginning the managed service team is at a disadvantage if it doesn't have the knowledge of the onshore team. While at the same early stage the extended team can rely on the experts in the onshore team to guide it through any complex issues. Thus the managed service team is reliant on the quality of transition that they made. If the onshore team is disbanded following the transition then they are on their own and have to find solutions to their own problems. So the full transition risk is high.

Hiring is very different in the two models. In the extended team the onshore manager will have the final say on all hires and no-one gets in without his agreement. This keeps the standards high but in my experience it has the unintended risk that teams don't grow fast enough because the onshore manager is not willing to let go and give more junior people in the offshore team a chance. When hiring, he tends to wait to find offshore candidates that are identical to his onshore team.

Conversely the managed service team is likely to have been constructed as a pyramid with fairly junior staff at the bottom. Once this model is working, adding more juniors is relatively easy compared to the flat extended team model where senior people are preferred.

Many offshore staff like working in a managed service team because they feel that they are playing an important role (high accountability) and they want to show that they can do well. I have seen staff from extended teams that had been itching to leave a company for years only to find that they readily accepted the challenge to move to a managed service team and then remained with the company for a long time to come. The pyramid structure is also an advantage in the managed service team as it gives staff a ladder to climb.

Staff members in the extended team don't feel the accountability of those in the managed service team and they notice their progress less as there is no ladder to climb. Despite this, they do have the advantage of working with the product experts onshore who may have 10 to 20 years' experience with that product or technology.

The service to be provided by the managed service team may be defined in a Service Level Agreement (SLA) or a software delivery contract. This is possible for a managed service team but not for an extended team because they don't deliver on their own, they are reliant on their onshore colleagues to collaborate with them to achieve their deliveries.

The management requirement above a collection of extended teams is different to that above a collection of managed service teams. There is a risk that the extended teams are managed so much from onshore that their senior management offshore becomes little more than administrators. On the other hand, managers of managed service teams are true delivery managers whose experience is needed to guide their teams towards results. These skills are more difficult to find.

Because the pyramid structure allows for the creation of teams containing junior staff with lower salaries, the result is likely to be a lower total staff cost than for the equivalent extended team. The managed service team also offers the possibility of transferring a complete piece of work offshore thus ensuring large cost savings with the elimination of the onshore team.

Despite the many advantages identified here for managed service teams, it is important to note that many Captive Centres have a high percentage of extended teams offshore. Their extended teams are productive and are contributing to significant cost savings. They remain extended teams due to perceived lack of skills offshore and the resultant high risk of transforming the team to a managed service. At the very least this model allows offshoring to start long before the whole team's business and product knowledge transfer is complete. Therefore, in a way, the extended team model is being used as a low risk introduction to offshoring that particular activity that could eventually lead to the creation of a managed service with a reduced transition period.

Scenario example 1.
Imagine an IT team in Germany that is responsible for building and maintaining a complex engineering software product. They have been told by their management that the product needs to expand to include more features but they will not have the budget to increase their local team. They will need to look at some form of offshoring. Every member of the IT team has at least 20 years of experience in IT and an average of 10 years' experience on this software product. This product requires a lot of engineering knowledge to understand it. The team has always recruited its own staff as juniors and helped them grow into more senior roles, given this experience they decide to create an extended team in their parent company's Captive Centre in India. They send a representative to India who screens candidates himself before deciding who can join the captive. When each person joins they are sent to Germany for 6 months of training. As a result of this investment in time and resources, the engineering software product team is successful in building an extended team of junior staff that they can manage from onshore.

Scenario example 2.
Alternatively, imagine the CIO of a company in Australia who needs to implement an e-commerce package and knows that it will require a significant amount of integration prior to delivery and then continual enhancements to keep the customer's attention for years to come. The e-commerce package is open source and he knows that there are many people on the market who have experience with it. For this implementation project, knowledge of how to integrate and customise the e-commerce package will be more important than knowing the company's business domain. The CIO decides to create a managed service team in the company's Captive Centre in China to build and maintain the e-commerce package. There was no existing team to extend and no reason why there would need to be a team onshore. The sales team will work directly with the managed service team to define the requirements for the e-commerce package. In practice the client of the managed service team will be the sales team and not the IT department. An SLA is signed between the new e-commerce team, the sales team and the CIO.

Product Oriented offshoring versus Technology oriented offshoring

For the purpose of this comparison imagine teams that manage a portfolio of IT projects based on the extended team model. In the product oriented case there is one team for each product within the portfolio and staff never move temporarily from one team to another. In the technology oriented case there is one pool of staff who are assigned, loosely, to a product oriented team. They are assigned loosely because after a management decision people working on product X could be re-assigned temporarily to work on product Y for a number of weeks or months. Thus staff really operate as part of a pool and are assigned to work as necessary. The time needed to establish these two types of team structures would be similar. Although there may be an advantage for the technology oriented team if they operate a staffing bench or if their dynamic of assigning people to different products is such that they become more experienced and more agile at accepting new products.

A typical extended product oriented team will take time to scale-up. In comparison a technology oriented team should be faster. This is because the technology oriented team has a greater degree of autonomy. If it has the right to add people at short notice then it will have greater flexibility over hiring in general than the product oriented team will. Of course it has to put processes in place to ensure it hires people with the right skills and who are fit for the team, but already being trusted to do so would be an advantage. Also during the scale-up period it is likely that the portfolio manager will assign existing staff from his pool (who may have never worked on this product) to now work on this product because the technologies are the same, this would save time too.

Staff turnover for a pure product oriented team is typically lower than for the technology oriented team. This is because the staff get involved with the business purpose of the product and build strong relationships with their onshore IT teams and users. The relationships built by the technology oriented teams are likely to be less strong because they can be re-assigned at any time and they don't believe that they are dedicated to one product.

A staff member who is only interested by technology might prefer a pure technology oriented team in which he may stay for a long time, but this sort of person is typically hired by software companies and not by offshore IT departments.

Full transition risk for business products is lower with a product oriented team because the staff that have been trained initially are tied to the product team. Therefore the loss of information or the loss of goodwill towards gaining that information is low. The technology oriented team may appear to start off this way but once staff get re-assigned to other products then the information is diluted and the offshore risk increases.

Full transition risk for simpler products, or where the documentation and degree of process is very high, would be similar for both teams. Being a technology oriented team will not provide any particular advantage to achieving a full transition.

To operate a pool and assign staff as necessary between product teams requires a higher level of autonomy and trust in offshore management than is required for a product oriented team.

The whole point of the technology oriented team structure is to be able to re-assign staff between teams as needed. Therefore if there is a resource peak requirement in one team while another team has staff underutilised (or the product work is declared to be a lower priority) then staff can be transferred temporarily or permanently. This is not possible with product oriented teams particularly if the technologies within the portfolio are different.

The technology oriented team allows for a different way of looking at a portfolio of work. It also has a higher degree of autonomy compared to a product oriented team. This combination is likely to lead to the identification of further transformations that could save cost. This might simply be by reducing the total number of people in the pool and then having less full time people assigned to each product, or it could be the merger of product teams or the elimination of similar IT products. The pure product oriented teams are unlikely to have this same vision as they are constrained by their product silos.

If these are extended teams then the accountability will be higher for the product oriented team. They will feel a degree of ownership for the one product on which they work and they will build good relationships with their onshore colleagues. This will not be possible to the same degree with the technology oriented team if they have not been hired for a specific product and if they are regularly moved. Alternatively, if they were both managed service teams then their accountability would be equally high.

In every organisation there are IT products and services provided directly to the big money makers of the business or perhaps to the big boss himself. For this type of VIP I would only ever offer a service from a product oriented team that is dedicated to his IT product.

The product oriented team knows that it has to do what is necessary to achieve the product work. If the product uses multiple technologies then they have to adapt to this and learn something about the technologies that are new to them. Technology oriented teams are likely to be a little less accepting of other technologies as they will see themselves as having invested in a particular technology and that is their career direction.

In the case of extended teams, the offshore manager of a technology oriented portfolio of teams has a greater autonomy in terms of hiring and allocating staff to product teams than the manager of a loose collection of product teams. Therefore it requires the portfolio manager to have the skills and experience to be autonomous. He will also need to be supported by his senior management as his staff allocation decisions may not always be popular. In contrast, for the managed service teams autonomy would have to be equally high for the technology or product oriented teams.

Often the main reason for building technology oriented teams is that the total cost would be lower than it would be for pure product oriented teams. In the beginning the costs may well be equal because the number of staff members needed for each team will have been strongly influenced by the onshore team managers. From this point on the local portfolio manager should be making the decisions about staff allocation and his aim will be to really understand the true demand and to see how he can allocate just enough people to provide the necessary level of service. His goal will be to try to reduce the overall cost without the true end users of the product noticing a reduction in service, even if the onshore team remains sceptical.

Scenario example 1.
Imagine the CIO of a Captive Centre in India with many IT teams. The business behind the product lines of the parent company are quite complicated and the IT teams are still expected to have their own strong business knowledge. Within the parent company the users expect everyone to already know what they know and they don't expect to have to explain anything twice. This culture permeates through to the onshore IT department and influences the way they are prepared to work with their offshore colleagues. The onshore IT team don't want to increase the maturity of the relationship they have with their extended teams if it means writing more documents and spending more time explaining what needs to be done, it is just not in their culture. Therefore the CIO of the Captive Centre makes the most of this by organising the management of his IT teams to be the mirror image of the onshore IT teams. This creates an environment of maximum integration between onshore and offshore teams for the same product areas. He knows it may not be the cheapest model but it is workable and manages to deliver major savings compared to having all the IT teams onshore.

Scenario example 2.
Alternatively, imagine the CIO of a different Captive Centre in India with many IT teams. In the last year he has been under extreme pressure to deliver certain applications on time that have slipped due to requirement misunderstandings, staff turnover and technology problems. More resources were needed to catch up on these applications but no extra budget was authorised. Knowing that the group CIO is going to visit the Captive Centre in the next few weeks, he takes the opportunity to review the management structure. He can see that the IT portfolio managers each have collections of products organised by business line or product line and that the technologies used are not the same. He prepares a presentation showing how he can re-organise these teams by grouping them into technology portfolios. This will allow him to pool the technical resources within a portfolio and redeploy them to the products that need extra resources for short periods of time without increasing the budget. The group CIO accepts this approach as he knows that the portfolios of IT activities offshore have now reached a level of maturity that they can make changes to the staffing without impacting productivity and he is pleased that there is now a solution to managing peak workloads.

Follow the Sun versus Centralisation

This comparison will consider the most common use for follow-the-sun versus centralisation which is to provide a 24 hour service for Application Production Support. The general themes should also be applicable to other types of 24 hour working.

Follow the sun requires teams in at least three locations around the world that hand over to each other to achieve a 24 hour service. Centralisation is the creation of one team that works in a shift pattern around the clock to provide a 24 hour service. For this comparison, assume that centralisation only takes place in the offshore centre.

The time required to put the initial staff structure in place is dependent on the starting point and how much of a transformation is planned. There are two main scenarios, either there are existing support teams in place already and they need to be transformed to achieve this service, or there are no teams in place (perhaps it is a new product) and therefore everyone needs to be hired.

Hiring the complete team in the global offshore centre will be faster than recruiting staff in each of the follow the sun locations. The offshore centre is built for this sort of ramp-up. In addition it will not be easy to coordinate the recruitment across multiple sites for follow the sun.

If there are existing teams in place already then it could be relatively quick to establish the follow the sun teams. In contrast, if the existing teams are in the wrong location, or there are too many people, or too many locations then a transformation will be needed and this will take time.

For much the same reasons it will be faster for the central team to scale-up than for each follow the sun team to scale up.

Staff turnover for centralisation will be higher than for follow-the-sun. This is for the simple reason that no-one likes working night shifts and they will do this only until they find a better opportunity. I personally recruited many good staff from offshore companies that insisted on forcing their staff to stay on night shifts. The new recruits saw the main selling point of moving companies as the opportunity to work normal hours again. Also, by definition, centralisation offshore will be away from the end user clients and having no contact with them can increase attrition over time.

Because bright ambitious people don't want to work night shifts for long, there is a greater risk of transitioning the complete support for an application to a centralised team, than with follow the sun. Also in the follow the sun model at least one of the locations used is likely to be close to the end users, this makes it easier to understand the business purpose of the product and to reduce the long term offshore risk.

The transition of well structured, fully documented "simple" products will work equally well in both scenarios.

With the whole activity centralised in one location it is easier to see the big picture and to identify further cost savings. In the follow the sun model it is more difficult to judge if the right number of resources are being allocated or not.

Accountability should be equal in both cases. However, if one or more of the locations are close to the end users and they build a good working relationship then accountability in that location will be higher.

If there are VIP clients then it is possible with the follow the sun model to ensure that there are some support staff physically near to them who can meet with them as necessary. This is not possible with the centralised model. Of course the centralised model can be sensitised for particular VIPs. In one case the onshore management issued the centralised team with a short list of the VIPs so that they could prioritise their support needs and it was effective.

For follow the sun there needs to be a team leader in each location and that team leader will have a local staff manager. In addition, somewhere in the world there will be a manager responsible for the complete follow the sun team who aims to take a global view.

Centralisation requires management who know how to manage a 24 hour activity with the local staff while not alienating the global end users. This is a specific skill set.

The centralised team will need to provide facilities for the staff working during the night. The Captive Centre will be in a developing country and the options for travel during the night will be limited. Therefore the offshore centre will need to provide a pick-up and drop-off service to ensure that its night staff travel safely. Night working staff will also require food and drink and therefore the staff canteen will need to stay open 24 hours too.

Despite the additional expenses for transport, food and drink the centralised support team should be significantly cheaper than the follow-the-sun team. This is because the centralised team consists entirely of staff from the Captive Centre who are cheaper than the staff in the onshore follow the sun locations.

Follow the sun could be implemented more cheaply if each of the regional teams was located within one of the organisation's regional offshore or near shore centres but this is rarely the case because product knowledge is better retained by keeping some of the staff that work near the end users and therefore not in an offshore location.

Scenario example 1.
Imagine a global company with headquarters in the United States that is implementing a new package system for IT security permission management and control. It will be integrated with legacy IT security systems, LDAPs, databases and other packages across the world in order to achieve the maximum automation of application permission requests. The trade-off for this automation will be the need to actively support the application 24 hours/day during the working week. The global CIO decides to deliver the 24 hour support from the company's Captive Centre in Mexico. This centralised model means that only one team needs to be trained in how to support the application and as everyone is offshore there will be significant cost savings. The central team will be guaranteed to use the same operating procedures throughout their day and therefore the users will benefit from a defined level of service at all times. Because the Captive Centre is often creating new teams, it is quick to build the new support team and is even able to include some support staff who have previous experience of using the same IT security package.

Scenario example 2.
Alternatively, imagine a different global company with headquarters in the United States that wants to reduce the total cost of ownership of an in-house application used for consolidation and reporting of P&L from subsidiaries across the world. The application is complicated and fragile. It is reliant on good quality feeds of data arriving on time in order to produce P&L reports for the senior management by the start of the day. Often a P&L error can only be fixed by refeeding files from the upstream systems. The support team has grown organically over the years as this application has become more critical to the user teams across the world. The operations teams for this application in each major location often visit the IT support team to discuss problems and work together on solutions. This works well as a follow the sun team. The IT support team structure ensures that there are staff in each major hub for the global organisation. The IT team has years of experience with this application and the quality of service would suffer if they were ever centralised.

Lift and Shift versus Fix and Shift

Many offshore transitions are vetoed because the activity is not considered ready for offshoring. This is because there are known problems with the activity and it is believed that the only transition technique is "fix and shift" where all the problems have to be fixed before transition. Often the main problem with fix and shift is allocating enough resources to resolve the problems. If offshoring is being considered then costs must already be tight and therefore asking for additional resources to solve the problems may well be rejected.

An alternative is "lift and shift". Here the offshore resources are used to resolve the problems. The biggest advantage of lift and shift is a much shorter time to start the transition project. The offshore centre can add more people to the activity at a much faster rate than the onshore team can.

During the transition to offshore there is a risk of staff turnover and valuable information needed for continuing the activity being lost. From experience I see a greater turnover risk in asking the existing onshore team to solve the problems that they have lived with for a long time, rather than having the offshore team do it. My preference is to keep the onshore team as stable as possible, still doing their daily job and allow the offshore team to do "lift and shift".

Of course there is a limit to how much of a mess can be offshored and the problems then resolved offshore. The greater the complexity of the activity and the products involved the greater the transition risk. Conversely it is necessary to consider how the onshore team have continued so long with this sub-optimal situation and to ask why the offshore team couldn't just start by doing the same thing.

Scenario example 1.
Imagine an application in a French company which has many support incidents every day. The onshore application support team know that the situation will not improve until the development team make some major improvements. Unfortunately the company is in the middle of a cost efficiency programme and there is no budget available to help the onshore application team improve the application. As part of the efficiency programme the IT application support team has already been targeted for offshoring. The Romanian offshore team meet with the IT team in France and discuss what the best approach would be. The onshore team are concerned that if the application is offshored as it is today then the application will continue to have many production incidents and senior management will believe that the offshoring was a failure. Following the meeting, the CIO of the Romanian Captive Centre makes a proposal to his counterpart in France that the best solution would be to "lift and shift". Both the application development team and the application support team should be offshored together. The lower development staff cost offshore would allow a temporary increase in staff numbers. These extra people could improve the application and thus reduce the long term support incidents. This is accepted and the offshore transition project is lengthened to allow time for the offshore improvements.

Scenario example 2.
Alternatively, imagine in a different French company that there is an application that generates many support incidents each day. The management want to reduce costs by offshoring to their Captive Centre but they also want to resolve the production problems with the application. After detailed analysis the exact problems with the application are identified and they are found to be in one module that manages the parallel loading of the external feeds. This is a complex piece of multi-threaded and multi-process code. To resolve the problem would require the expertise of a system programmer not an application programmer. The head of their Romanian Captive Centre admits that he does not have a systems programmer of this kind available. Therefore it is decided that it would be best to "fix and shift", to let the current onshore team resolve the problems with the loading module before offshoring the application. Once complete, this module should never need to be touched again and so the offshore team shouldn't even need to be trained in it.

Fixed price engagement versus time and materials

For this comparison imagine two managed service projects with an outsourcing vendor, one is fixed price and the other time and materials. Although in practice the supplier could be a profit centre Captive instead.

It would be quicker to start the time and materials engagement. This is because an estimate of the total cost is all that is needed to get approval and therefore the risk may be taken of not having completed the requirements analysis to the finest level of detail. The client knows that it can change the requirements later on if really necessary. In comparison, the client of the fixed price engagement cannot negotiate the contract until it knows exactly what service is to be delivered. Once the supplier has started on the fixed price engagement they will continue until they have either delivered what was documented in the contract or the client interrupts them to negotiate a change in the deliveries.

For the same supplier, the time taken to scale up the two teams, the turnover of the staff and the full transition risk should be identical. This is assuming that the vendor would have chosen the composition of both teams to be the same and he was not influenced by the client in the selection of the T&M team.

The client should not expect the supplier to communicate further ideas, transformations or improvements once the fixed price contract has started. In contrast, the same supplier may identify and implement improvements in a T&M engagement. These improvements may increase or decrease the total T&M invoicing. The client's onshore management need to be experienced in fixed price supplier management. They need to know how to do their own accurate cost estimation in order to verify the supplier's quotation. Above all they need to prepare as much as possible to be able to define the delivery completely before signing the contract. For the T&M engagement the onshore management has flexibility to change the deliveries once the project has started.

In a fixed price engagement the client will never know if the supplier underruns on the cost he quoted or overruns. The savings or overspend will not be passed on to the client unless they are enormous (e.g. more than 25% of the total cost). For a T&M engagement the client pays for the days the staff were engaged and the expense of their materials. Of course the unit cost the client pays for the staff will be higher than the cost to the supplier who will be expecting to make a profit out of the engagement.

If after either engagement has started, the client realises that the definition of the deliveries must change then he can issue a change request. At this point the supplier of the fixed price engagement will always charge the client for requesting a change even if it reduces the scope of the delivery, this is normally how the contract is written. The only exception will be if a certain number of change requests had already been paid for in the contract. The same change request received by the T&M engagement will be included and the invoicing will adjust itself depending on whether more or less days were spent on the delivery.

The most difficult question to answer is whether overall the fixed price engagement will save the client money or not. Conceptually, an IT manager would expect the fixed price engagement to equal the cost of the T&M engagement plus a buffer for unexpected occurrences. It can then be inferred that if there was no risk in the engagement and no changes were requested then the fixed price engagement would be more expensive. In practice there will be many risks and many change requests, understanding these is the key to understanding which will be the cheapest option. Typically a client would choose a fixed price engagement because they can't accurately predict these risks and therefore instead they prefer to pass these risks on to the supplier in return for having a fixed cost to pay.

Scenario example 1.
Imagine a company in England that needs to develop a new mobile phone application. Their marketing department has written a clear presentation stating what their requirements are for the application. The IT team has spent a few days with the marketing team and as a result has been able to write a detailed functional specification document which has been approved by the marketing department. They are in no doubt as to what the application needs to do. Despite this, they know that they don't have the resources in-house to build the application and if they were to wait while a team was built then they would lose the business opportunity. With a functional specification available they are able to ask a number of offshore vendors to provide them a fixed price quote for doing the work. They compare the quotes and decide to give the business to an outsourcing vendor in Poland because they believe that the proximity will help resolve any misunderstandings and keep them within the agreed fixed price contract. The business management is pleased with this because it means that the IT costs within the new business programme are now fixed and the major risk of IT project cost overrun has been eliminated.

Scenario example 2.
Alternatively, imagine a different company in England that needs to develop a new corporate website complete with dynamic content and links to external cloud services. The marketing department have written a presentation of what they want to see in the new corporate website. Unfortunately, when the IT team start to work with the marketing team they realise that their ideas are not fully developed and the marketers imply that the functional specification may need to change in six months but they are not sure. Furthermore, when the IT team looks in detail at the external cloud services they get the impression that the services are not mature and they fully expect interface revisions in the near future. As a result of this uncertainty the company looks for vendors that will offer a time and materials development contract. They are able to estimate the number of man/years for the specified project, and hence to calculate what the vendor's final bill will be, but they expect the requirements to change. When they meet with different vendors they are not able to negotiate a fixed price, and therefore they can only negotiate on the cost per man/day. The company chooses a Polish outsourcing vendor that they believe is close enough that they can be available for discussion throughout the working day and they could visit each other to discuss the requirements when they change.

~~

How to source Captive Centre staff

Staff Lead time

If you don't have the staff available in the Captive Centre then you are going to need to either recruit them from the market or engage them from a vendor.

If the outsourcing vendor has the type of staff you want waiting on the bench then the shortest lead time would be to take these people. Alternatively, if the vendor doesn't have the staff immediately available or there is a reason why you don't believe that their available staff can do the job, then you need to look at recruiting staff from the market.

The vendor may propose that he recruits the staff into his organisation for your use. This can work but be careful that he doesn't recruit staff that you then reject. He won't recruit staff that meet your specific criteria alone, he will look for good long term staff for his organisation. This immediately puts a ceiling on their compensation as well. An alternative could be to propose to the vendor that the recruitment drive takes place in your Captive Centre with his recruitment team and yours in attendance. This may avoid the vendor recruiting staff that you later reject.

Recruiting your own permanent staff has the longest lead time but can be the most rewarding. To estimate the lead time don't just think about how long it will take to identify the candidates and conduct the interviews, make sure you know what the average notice period is in that location. For example, in India today almost all staff are on a 3 month notice period.

Staff Engagement Cost

Vendor staff in their own premises or your own permanent staff in your premises will cost you a similar amount and will be the cheapest option.
The more expensive option is to use the vendor's staff in your own offices. This comes at a premium as you will have to contribute to the cost of the infrastructure the person uses. In the first case the outsourcing vendor will have included this in the cost.

Long term planning

Remember that vendor staff will not stay with you forever. The outsourcing vendor will have promised a long term career plan and the next step on the ladder is unlikely to be at the same client's organisation. After being engaged by your organisation for at least 1 year expect any day that vendor staff will give you notice.

Your own permanent staff will have accepted, to a degree that the level of career planning for them will be less than the vendor will offer so they should not be disappointed. However, you will still need to make sure that they get offered opportunities if you want them to grow and stay.

Technologies will change over the long term. Therefore in-house permanent staff will eventually need to be retrained. This problem is managed for you if you use vendor staff only and you allow them to rotate.

Quality

Many outsourcing vendors have excellent staff. They have a lot to offer candidates and therefore they can attract good talent. Despite this, you can't be sure that the vendor will offer you the best people just because he has them. He is most likely to offer you candidates who are just good enough for your needs.

The reason for this is that he can make more money using his expert staff for his own purposes than he can by contracting them to you. By way of example, consider that he has an architect who could either work for you on a daily fixed rate or he could be supporting ten different teams to deliver lucrative fixed price contracts.

When you recruit your own staff then you control the quality. That is assuming that you have an attractive enough proposition to receive applications from high quality candidates.

Remember that in the offshoring model, you only need staff that are good enough to do the job that they are being recruited for. In Western countries the tendency is to "over recruit" and bring in people that might run the IT department one day. This is counterproductive in the offshoring model.

Methodologies

All tier-1 offshore vendors are CMMi 5 accredited. They have strong in-house processes and methodologies. They will also have specific tools and processes for offshore transition, building new applications, testing applications and transforming legacy applications. In-house IT departments are unlikely to have such a complete set of processes, tools or the culture to use them. Therefore you might imagine that by engaging outsourcing vendor staff you would be getting all of this body of knowledge too and it would help make your IT offshoring a success.

This would be true if you asked the vendor to conduct the IT activity at his own premises using a managed service model so that he has complete autonomy. Unfortunately, if you ask his staff to come and work in your own premises then all you get is the people you have engaged. Whether this is true because the outsourcing vendor staff no longer have access to their internal tools or a different reason remains to be seen.

In summary, if you want to benefit from particular methodologies then you either need to have them available in your Captive Centre (for in-house or vendor staff) or you need to let the vendor do the work at his premises.

Attrition

There is a risk of attrition with internal and external staff. However, the risk with the vendor resources working in your Captive Centre is more pronounced. The external staff will quickly learn that they are being underpaid compared to your internal staff. Then when a staff-member resigns from the vendor, they try to "manage" the situation for a few weeks before telling the client. So the client ends up with very little notice before the vendor resource leaves.

Your own permanent staff have to tell you when they want to leave, so you get the longest possible notice as per the contract that they signed.

Vendor employees can become most restless in the build up to bonus payments being made to the permanent staff within the Captive Centre. Any bonus paid by the vendor is likely to be less than the average paid by the Captive Centre and yet during the build up to the bonus period at the Captive Centre the vendor staff will find that their colleagues can talk of nothing else. We should not forget either that the outsourcing vendor rotating his staff to another client feels like attrition for the current client even if it is not counted as such by the vendor.

Permanent Professional hire

It will be impossible to transition complete activities (a full transition) to the Captive Centre unless you have good senior staff in the organisation. These people come ready packaged with the knowledge, skills and experience to take on major tasks and to help others achieve their tasks.

If you can't find people like this in the local market then the type of IT work that can be offshored will be very restricted.
I have witnessed this situation first hand in a country that was new to IT offshoring and was producing good new graduates. Unfortunately, there were no senior staff available on the market because IT on a large scale was still new. As a result the organisation had to recruit everyone as graduates and train them. This meant that they were restricted to basic software maintenance and support activities that required an average of no more than 2 years' experience.

The downside of hiring this ready packaged senior ability is that there might be a mismatch somewhere else in their profile other than their technical skills.

An example of this is hiring senior staff with IT product development experience versus IT project experience. Both require good technical skills. But these are not the same mind set. The product developer thinks about the long term evolution of what he is building, while the project oriented developer is used to meeting the project deadlines at all costs.

Graduates

Graduate entry staff are the life blood of the tier-1 IT outsourcing vendor companies. They take in far more graduates each year than they do senior hires.

I thoroughly recommend having a yearly graduate recruitment programme as part of the official strategy. In lean years you may not hire a large number of graduates and you may well still hire more senior staff each year.

Fresh graduates have many advantages. They are keen and want to make their mark, so they will really put effort into whatever you ask them to do. Normally they have a lot of energy and a big capacity for work, so you can give them a large task to do and watch as they take it on to completion. They can be trained and moulded to fit a particular organisation, thus avoiding the culture clash that can happen with senior hires. After they have been trained then quite quickly they will catch up with their immediate seniors in many tasks, this creates a healthy professional competition. I also find that they remain open to technologies and job roles that many seniors aren't willing to transfer to due to the investment that they have already made in one technology.

Having a yearly graduate programme requires investment as these people may not be fully productive for 6 months. So, if this is a cost centre model then it is necessary to get the buy-in of the parent organisation and convince them that they need to spend money on this. Such a decision requires a long term vision of staffing requirements in the Captive Centre and hence a good estimate of the offshore targets beyond the next 2 years. A profit centre captive may make an internal decision to hire graduates each year and then fund it from its own profits.

Many agencies and HR consultancies have graduate recruitment teams allowing you to subcontract or outsource your graduate recruitment to them. In a country that has a large number of universities with a huge potential number of eligible graduates then you often need help with recruitment. They will target particular universities for you. Then they can organise candidate testing for you. It is necessary to write the tests and then the agency will conduct them. If the tests were multiple choice they will get them marked and send you the CVs of the candidates with the best results. Only at this stage do you then need to involve your own staff and have them interview the final candidates. This service can achieve a significant cost and time saving over using your own technical, management and HR staff.

Once you have your new graduates remember that they don't want you to take it easy on them. They will have joined your organisation because they want to make progress in their careers. In the first few years after graduation they will not expect a good work/life balance. Make sure their skills are fully employed or else they are likely to leave.

Vendor staff offshore body shopping

Many outsourcing companies don't advertise that they body shop their staff to their clients as it is a low value add business model for them. They can make more money selling services.

Despite this, body shopping can be a quick way to reduce your lead time to offshore an activity. The outsourcing vendor could be asked to supply a whole team or to provide staff for particular roles that would work in a hybrid team with in-house staff. The vendor staff will expect to work in your Captive Centre in the same way as your in-house staff. This means that they will be willing to follow your internal procedures and try to fit in culturally.

After a few weeks it won't be obvious that they are vendor staff. The downside of this arrangement is that they won't bring the procedures and processes with them that have made their employer a successful offshore business.

Furthermore it may not be productive to ask them their opinion on the processes you intend to use as they would have been reliant on a dedicated department to create the processes for them. No-one would ever have asked them their opinion on the subject before.

Vendor staff managed service

Your office

Unless your outsourcing vendor already has a network connection to your organisation (e.g. they have a dedicated ODC already) then the quickest way to get a team working is to put them in your Captive Centre premises. As was mentioned in another section, expect this option to be marginally more expensive than using your own in-house staff as this is not the vendor's preferred business model.

Even though you are expecting an industrialised process, the problems stated above for body shopping regarding tools and processes still remains for a managed service in your office. They will probably be more willing to use some of their tools but it will be difficult if they don't have access to their own networks.

However, if they do manage to use some of their processes then you should expect regular visits from staff you have not paid for or regular trips back to base for the team. This is because their process model expects their experts to review their decisions and their work at regular intervals. This is an advantage but remember that is also being done to allow for slighter lower experienced staff to be assigned to your activity.

The managed service team will do everything they can to fit into the culture of your office. This is the best thing that can happen, you don't want them to appear separate from the rest of the teams as this will create rumours and unrest.

Similarly, you should invite them to staff meetings and social functions both to help them integrate and also to demonstrate to your permanent staff teams that you already consider the vendor staff to be part of the organisation.

Their office

If the vendor does any managed service work from their office then remember that you won't really be managing them as staff. Be prepared to write a good SLA or project delivery contract through which you can manage them.

Be prepared to make it clear who they report to: either the onshore management or the offshore management in the captive centre. Remember that they might not see the offshore management team adding much value. So you have to first be clear how it is going to work and then to tell them.

This arrangement will then proceed similar to subcontracting. So it will be necessary to define plans, set milestones and define KPIs so that their progress can be tracked and managed.

They will have full access to their own processes and tools from their office. Ask them which processes they intend to use and why. Early agreement is needed to avoid disappointment. If you know which process they are using then it will make it easier to follow their work.

Vendor lead time risks

The biggest lead time issue is connectivity from the outsourcing vendor's office to the client organisation.

Assuming this is achieved, then the next biggest lead time will be the creation of the team and any recruitment that is needed.

Remember that this is a managed service and so you must let the vendor decide the composition of his own team and then manage him on his deliveries. Of course if you are concerned then you can always ask them to present what they believe the team structure should be and why, or you could insist that certain skills need to be within the team (but not in each individual).

Recruiting the Vendor's staff

When the vendor's staff are working within your premises you may find that some of the staff are so good that you can't bare letting them rotate off to another client, or perhaps through misfortune they are now the only staff in the world who know how to execute your IT activity. It would be human nature to try to recruit them from the vendor and make them permanent staff within your Captive Centre.

Take heed, in developing countries it is rare for the outsourcing vendor to ever let you recruit his staff that he has lovingly nurtured. Even after your senior management threaten to break off the relationship with the vendor you will still be lucky to get agreement for even one person to be recruited. Don't forget that the staff may also be quite happy working for the vendor. You may propose them a little more money but they may be waiting for a major promotion with their company.

Normally the first response from the supplier will be that they have processes and procedures to ensure an efficient hand over of knowledge between their staff. Therefore, according to them, the departure risk that you perceive does not exist and they can introduce replacement or additional staff and train them at any time. This may even be enough.

If you do succeed in getting agreement from the vendor then don't expect any more than the right to put your case to their employee. The vendor will never go so far as to agree that you can actually hire their employee, it would have to be the employee's choice.

This section may be hard to believe for you or for your onshore senior management. I have been in this situation many times and I am sure that each time the onshore managers didn't understand the situation and thought that I was just not trying hard enough. In the western world, and especially in central Europe, it is normal to body shop a resource and if he is good then to pay a recruitment fee (or penalty amount) to the supplier. Once achieved the contractor is then recruited as a new employee. I have never heard of this happening amicably in developing countries.

At one organisation they wrote in the contract with their vendors that any staff who stayed more than 18 months would become eligible to be approached for recruitment. This was accepted by the outsourcing vendor during a moment of business weakness. However, as soon as the market turned up the vendor simply rotated its key staff onto new clients before the 18 month eligibility was reached. As a result few recruitments ever took place.

The only guaranteed transfer of staff from an outsourcing vendor to a client is through an official BOT (Build Operate and Transfer) contract. Even with this model I would expect the client to pay more than if it did the recruitment from the market itself and I wouldn't expect all of the key vendor staff to remain in the organisation any longer by the time the transfer stage is reached.

Freelance staff

In developing countries freelance staff are very rare. People need financial security and therefore prefer to be employed by a stable organisation.

Saying that, I have found a limited number of good freelance staff in these countries by word of mouth that have made a great contribution.

Freelance staff tend to be experts in a particular niche rather than simply generalists. This can be very useful in the right circumstances.

Temporary staffing agencies

In developing countries the temporary employment agencies tend to provide the staff that can't get employed anywhere else. If you have a simple process oriented role in a mature area and you need staff quickly at a low cost then this might be a reasonable choice.

The advantage is that they would be ready immediately and could be laid off immediately. These are the only types of roles I would consider temporary agencies for.

Skills availability: understanding the history

The skills available in a particular developing country are strongly linked to the commercial history of that country. If you are targeting a large country, such as India, then the history needs to be also considered city by city.

Skills availability: Legacy Skills

Mass IT offshoring is probably fairly new to the developing country you have targeted. Offshoring probably started there on a large scale no more than 15 years ago and perhaps as few as 5 years ago.

Legacy systems are by definition old. So how are you going to find experienced people to work on your legacy systems that you want to offshore?

Start by looking at the history of the country. Did they have an IT business of some kind before mass offshoring started? For instance, there are parts of India where IBM had a strong presence a long time ago. Consequently in these areas there are still good IBM mainframe skills to be found.

Perhaps on a smaller scale, consider which companies were present in that country a long time ago. Were there any IT companies? Or if there were big non-IT companies, did they have IT departments and what type of technologies did they use? Alternatively, what type of IT systems were used by the central government or schools?

Failing that, since the time of mass offshoring in this country, is there one company that has already offshored the technology that you need? It may be possible to convince some of their current or ex-employees to join your Captive Centre.

Skills availability: Mainstream Skills

If a country has been providing offshoring for the last 10 years then it is likely to have skills in all the mainstream technologies that have been used in that period.
Be careful about the availability of trained staff on expensive technologies. In a developing country the cost of the licences may be significant. If you look at the technical universities you will probably see that they all teach JAVA but few of them teach Microsoft. Licence cost matters and it is still reflected in the availability of skilled staff years later.

Skills availability: Leading Edge Skills

To find staff experienced in leading edge skills you will need to find companies that embrace leading edge technologies. It is unlikely that the universities will have found it necessary to update their teaching with the very latest technologies, so they won't be leading the way.

Look for areas that have attracted captive centres for companies that do leading edge technologies. Examples would include Google, Yahoo or Microsoft who have all had offshore activities at some point in time.

Skills availability: Learning the Skills

If you can't find the skills that you are looking for, and you are convinced that you shouldn't re-write the system in something more mainstream, then you will need another solution.

The ultimate solution is to find willing participants and to train them in the technology. You could hire your own staff and do this or give the whole assignment to a vendor who will probably have done it before with a similar technology and therefore has learnt from the experience.

~~~

Recruiting permanent staff for the Captive Centre

Permanent Recruitment Process

Every organisation will have a different recruitment process. As an example, here is a fairly simple process that I have seen used before.

1. Write the job specification.
2. Agree the job specification with all parties.
3. Confirm that the recruitment is within budget.
4. HR send the job specification to the preferred list of agencies.
5. Receive CVs from the agencies and start screening.
6. Candidates who's CVs pass initial screening are invited for technical interviews.
7. Those passing the technical interview get a management interview.
8. Those passing the management interview get an HR interview and if successful an offer in principle during the same meeting.
9. HR send the candidate for a medical assessment and start an independent reference check.
10. Candidate accepts the offer and resigns from his current employer.
11. Candidate serves his notice period at his current employer.
12. Candidate joins his new employer.

External Agencies

You will need to build good working relationships with external recruitment agencies to recruit good permanent staff for the Captive Centre. This will be necessary for recruitment stakeholders: the HR recruitment team, the Captive Centre manager and the hiring managers.

The majority of the agencies in a developing country will be little more than "database" agencies. That is to say that they receive CVs from people, they store them on their database and then when you ask for candidates to match your profile they simply do a search on their database and send you the matching candidates. They may have never even met any of the candidates they are sending you or taken the time to find out if the people really exist let alone if their experience is real.

Build relationships with agencies that take more responsibility for the candidates they supply and are pro-active in finding the right candidates for you. They will need to "head hunt" when necessary by being prepared to target particular companies and cold call candidates. They also need the gumption and energy to follow up on the leads you give them and the leads they get from their work.

If you are going to do a lot of recruitment over a long period of time then I suggest that you introduce yourself to these agencies and make sure that they know your requirements. Leave the door open for them to come back and contact you whenever they need to. Note that many HR departments will not like this, typically they own the recruitment process, they manage the relationships with the external agencies and they don't want conflicting instructions to be given. In this case, restrict yourself to discussing existing roles and insist that any decisions or new candidate CVs continue to be sent through the official channels.

If you have a large requirement or a limited time to build a critical team then consider inviting all the preferred external agencies together to a meeting. Invite the HR team and the recruiting managers. Walk through the job requirements with everyone. Make sure there is no divergence in understanding what needs to be done. Ask the agencies to state their action plans.

Internal Agencies

Many of the large offshore centres that I was fortunate to be invited to, also had their own recruitment agencies internally. You may be thinking that this is the same as your HR department but it is not. Your HR department is unlikely to start cold calling candidates.

These successful offshore companies recruited a small number of external recruitment consultants and used them to close positions that they were finding difficult with their external preferred supplier list. So they were not putting them in competition with the external suppliers and they never intended to have enough of these staff internally to replace the external agencies.

Job advertisements

Placing an advert in the national or trade specific newspapers seems like a logical way to attract the right talent.
My personal experience of this in India is that you have to be prepared to invest a lot of time and even then you may have wasted your effort. However, advertising in these newspapers raises the profile of the organisation and the Captive Centre which is a benefit.

The problem in India is that the number of replies you will receive to a targeted advert will be huge. Perhaps in the hundreds or thousands. As many as 20% of the replies will come from candidates who seem to have not read the advert at all and are simply replying with their fingers crossed. Then the remaining 80% of the candidates will claim to have the experience you are looking for. Then comes the hard part, what can you do if you are facing the task of interviewing a few hundred candidates that all claim to have the right technical skills as per their CV history and covering letter? You will have no choice at this stage but to ask your technical teams to read the CVs and try to eliminate as many as possible. The remaining candidates can then be given a written test and anyone who passes will then get a face to face interview.

There are HR consultancy companies that will help with this process. Their real value is during the early filtering stage. So defining the test and then conducting the interviews will have to be run by your technical staff.

Recruitment drive versus daily search

You will need to involve your own technical staff at some point in the recruitment cycle. They will not accept someone into their team if they have not had any involvement in their recruitment. Even when you have technical test papers to be given to candidates and recruitment staff with some IT knowledge your technical teams will still need to get their hands dirty in recruitment.

The problem is that this takes a lot of time out of your team that they could have been spending on "billable" activities. So the question arises, is it better that they take time out every day to screen candidates or that they come back at weekends for a concentrated push? Personally I have found the most effective approach to be to start with the daily screening, follow up on their progress and if they are not closing the roles to then set a date for a weekend recruitment drive.

To make the drive effective you will need to invite the external recruitment agencies, the internal technical team and the HR team giving them as much notice as possible. If there is not a long queue of candidates then the recruitment agency needs to be tasked with having a good pipeline by the target date. Never run the recruitment drive without your HR team being present or else you won't be able to make offers to the candidates on the same day and this is what they have come for. Everyone wants the deal closed in that one day.

Staff referral

This is a great way to get quality staff that fit with the organisation. First you need to share the open positions with your staff that you want to recruit for. Then you ask them to name friends or former colleagues that match the criteria and would be interested in those roles. If a staff member refers someone in this way, and they are recruited, then they need to be rewarded either through management recognition or by a small monetary bonus.

Remember that you are saving paying a significant recruitment fee to an external agency so you can afford to pay a reward to the employee.

The referred candidate then gets interviewed and tested in the same way as any other candidate except that I would personally prioritise his interviews and I would make sure that the referring employee can't influence the outcome.

Within the organisations that I know, when the "hit rate" is compared for staff referrals compared to external market recruitment, the staff referrals always have a higher hit rate. That is proof that you waste less of your time on filtering referrals for recruitment than candidates on the market.

Employees need to be well informed on recruitment requirements for this method of recruitment to remain effective.

Lead-time

Recruiting permanent staff will take time. There could be delays at any one of the steps in the process.

In my personal experience the biggest delay occurs when the candidate doesn't show up for work on the first day and you have to start again, the second longest delay is when the candidate serves his notice period and the third longest delay can be getting the availability from the technical team to process the whole list of candidates (which could be long) in the first place.

If the notice period is 3 months long then you need to plan for the whole process taking 6 months.

Over recruitment

It is normal in the west to recruit the very best staff that can be found with the most future potential possible. It is rare to recruit someone who is a good fit for the current role without thinking what to do with them afterwards. In a developing country where the job market is liquid then you don't need to be concerned about employees staying beyond the life of their useful skills. They will move of their own accord if they know that they are no longer wanted.
You will want the right person for the job in your Captive Centre, you are prepared to pay for employees that have future career potential to grow and stay with the company. At the same time you also want to have team stability and to manage your costs. So you make sure that you hire the right person for the job. You don't hire someone who is so over qualified or over experienced that you pay a fortune for them or that they will be bored in 3 months and will want to move to another employer.

If you recruit someone who is too experienced or clearly too ambitious for the role then this is called "over recruitment" and it is best to avoid it.

One of the causes of over recruitment is having poor job descriptions. For example, stating on a job description document that a programmer needs to have 10 years of JAVA experience is not useful. It is necessary to think about what the person really needs to be able to do and to write this in the job description; e.g. which libraries, which frameworks, real time or batch processing experience. This will make it a lot easier to identify the right person.

Seniority costs

In a job market that is full of young people with limited experience, there is a cost for attracting senior staff. Salaries are not just slightly higher for senior staff in this type of market, salaries increase by multiples between junior and senior staff. Really accomplished senior IT managers will be paid not far from their western colleagues due to the rarity of their skills in that market.

Joining risks

In a very liquid market the candidates that have signed contracts with you may never arrive on their joining date. This is particularly true in India.

Candidates can find an upside in serving long notice periods by using this time to their advantage to identify an even better role than the one they have contractually committed to start. Once they have an offer from a company they can use this offer as the starting point for negotiations with yet another organisation. Therefore by following this process they are able to offer themselves to potential employers with less than their full notice period as they will have already resigned knowing that they have at least one job to go to. They may also manage to get a salary increase on top of the new (already increased) salary offered to them by the first company.

From my experience in India, this clever bargaining is available to everyone who wants to play the game but it is never any reflection on how long the candidate will stay with you once they have joined. So it is not an indicator of restlessness.

One form of protection the Captive Centre can use in these situations is to separate the offer letter from the appointment letter. In the final interview the candidate will only be given an offer letter which fully documents the offer he has discussed with HR but with the minimum of additional details. This is a legal offer and will be enough to allow him to resign from his employer.

Then, only when he joins his new employer on the first day of work will he receive a full letter with all of his appointment details.

What attracts offshore staff?

No one attribute of a role holds the same attraction for every possible candidate. Even an upper quartile salary will not satisfy all candidates.

In a developing country these can be the major points of attraction for a job role.

- Financial compensation
- Brand value
- Job title

- Overseas opportunities
- Good technologies
- Quality work
- Managed career path
- Good training
- Employer stability

Financial compensation includes salary, bonus or profit share. Many employers will convert this into an equivalent cash amount for the purposes of discussion with a candidate, even though in practice the candidate would never receive this amount in cash as it will be delivered by different compensation mechanisms throughout the year.

Perceived brand value is not only what the candidate thinks about the brand but what the candidate believes other people think about the brand. For example, will it look good on my CV, will it help get the next job, and will it impress my peers?

The quality of work is considered to be attractive if it is work that other people would want to do, or work in which new skills will be learnt that can be used to get a better job with another employer. For example, consider the difference in work quality between green field development projects versus maintenance of legacy applications.

It is quite common in outsourcing vendor organisations for staff to be given titles that are elevated compared to their real responsibilities. For example, someone may be designated project manager but they never manage projects. This promotion can be worth a lot to the employee lifting him up in the eyes of his social circle but beware as it creates mistrust with onshore clients who don't see it as being particularly honest.

Consider the value of your organisation's brand through the eyes of the candidate. An acclaimed brand in Germany might not be recognised at all by an IT candidate and their family in a developing country.

~~~

Why internal staff need redeployment

Willingness to redeploy

In developed countries I have observed a reticence among employees to move to new teams or to take on new responsibilities. It is as if the role they have needs protecting and will not easily be bettered.

In developing countries people know that they have to move to take the next step in their career. Therefore they find it a lot easier to accept redeployment and even cherish the experience. I have known staff who have happily trained and handed over their responsibilities to another employee in anticipation of being given a better role when they hadn't yet been told what the next role would be. This would be unthinkable onshore.

Career progression

Offshore staff expect to be redeployed to make progress in their career. Therefore it is necessary to either plan for these redeployments and then move staff as agreed, or communicate early on why a transfer can't take place for another few years.

Attrition reduction

Redeployment can be a strong aid to reducing the risk of attrition. Teams change regularly, they are created, merged, split and finally disbanded. Instead of recruiting new teams from outside the organisation, existing internal staff should be given the opportunity to apply for roles in these changing teams.
The best approach is not only to internally advertise the roles in the new team, but to be more pro-active and approach permanent staff that you believe would fit the role and ask them to apply. This helps the employees to know that you are thinking about them and that you have an interest in their career. Even asking targeted employees to apply, without them being accepted for the role, can be a tonic for their morale.

To be clear, I am not proposing the industrial scale staff rotations after a short period in a team that may happen within a vendor organisation. Instead I propose a light approach where people can stay for as long as they want within one team and the management also offers them opportunities to move.

~~~

Activity Full transition to offshore

The challenge

This section will explore the considerable challenge of moving a complete activity from an onshore location to an offshore location. It is more difficult to achieve than the creation of an extended team and has a greater risk of failure. In addition, time is usually limited in comparison to an extended team creation. Once the full transition is announced to the existing team then the clock is ticking to complete the work before key members of the onshore team decide to jump ship and take their knowledge with them.

Skills and Knowledge Matrices

The onshore team is a collection of different people with different skill sets and different levels of knowledge. The offshore team also has skills and knowledge. What is needed is a way of measuring the onshore skills, the offshore skills and then charting a course to close the gaps.

Skills and knowledge matrices help to do this. The key to understanding the problem is that all the skills present in the combined onshore team do not need to be present in every offshore team member.

Each onshore team member will be interviewed to determine what skills and knowledge they believe are needed to achieve the key activities of the team. These items need to be grouped into logical categories, e.g. front end skills, back end skills etc. This will form one axis of the matrix. Next the team members need to rate themselves for each of the knowledge areas and skills. This completes the first draft of the matrix which can then be reviewed, and corrected, with the onshore team manager.

In order to know the starting point, the offshore team members then need to be rated against the same knowledge areas and skills. This will complete the offshore team current state matrix.

It can save a lot of trouble later on if the onshore ratings are normalised before analysing the onshore to offshore knowledge and skill gaps. First of all there is a risk that the onshore team will have exaggerated their own skills.

Secondly the intention is not to build an offshore team that is identical to the onshore team, instead the transition manager needs to know what skill level would be enough to take responsibility offshore. The normalisation process can be carried out between the onshore and offshore managers, with additional staff interviews as necessary.

With the two matrices complete, it will be possible to see straight away where the offshore team has gaps in its knowledge and skills.

To achieve the offshore transition, it is enough for each skill category to have 2 people in the offshore team who are competent. So the next step is to assign offshore team members to the categories that need to be closed. Then organise these tasks into a targeted knowledge transfer (KT) plan.

KT: Approach

Knowledge Transfers (KT) must always be planned for in detail if they are to be successful. The onshore and offshore teams must have both reviewed the plan and agreed it. The onshore team needs to commit to being available at the dates and times written in the plan to transfer their knowledge.

From experience I have seen the most effective knowledge transfers being achieved by onshore teams that already had a new joiner process. Typically this process will have already been used a number of times and it would have benefited from the feedback of the earlier participants and improved.

Just like any project activity, it is advised to break the knowledge transfer up into different phases. In this way it is possible to measure whether a phase has been completed, if the offshore staff have reached their learning goal for that phase and therefore if the knowledge transfer is on target or not. Time is limited and therefore it is critical to have an early warning of any knowledge transfer problems.

Remember that even if you recruit someone who has come from doing an identical role at a competitor that he will still need to follow the Knowledge Transfer process in order to understand your systems and your way of working.

KT: Reading the Documentation

The most frequent way of transferring knowledge is to ask the offshore team to read any existing documents.

The advantage of this approach is that it takes no time away from the onshore team, therefore it can happen immediately and the onshore team's work will not be disrupted.

The disadvantage is that there is no guarantee that the documents are up to date or that they cover the complete scope of the activity.

KT: Classroom training

The classical approach to any learning activity is to hold classroom sessions. This requires the onshore team to prepare teaching materials (e.g. slide presentations) that can be used in a classroom with the offshore staff.

The advantage of this type of knowledge transfer is that a large number of people can be trained at the same time. The disadvantage of classroom training is the time it takes to prepare the teaching material and someone needs to be experienced enough and confident enough to conduct the classroom training. Also classroom training is not very interactive and so it is difficult to know whether the knowledge has been absorbed or not. From experience I would advise setting the classroom students with a short test, a quiz or some homework every day to make sure they are absorbing the information and are able to apply it.

KT: Write your own documentation

An alternative approach to knowledge transfer is to ask the offshore team to prepare their own documentation for the software product itself and on the processes to be followed. This puts the emphasis on the offshore team to ask the right questions of the onshore team. To help them they should use a good analysis template so that they don't miss any major points. Once the offshore team have some of the documentation ready then they must ask the onshore team to review it, make corrections and offer improvements.

The advantage of this approach is that it makes less demands on the onshore team compared to classroom training and it relies on the professionalism of the offshore team. Also it doesn't require the onshore team to possess any classroom teaching skills.
The disadvantage is the reliance on the offshore team doing a thorough job and the difficulty to include large numbers of people in the analysis unless it can be easily split up into separate chunks.

KT: Job shadow and reverse job shadow

This is a very hands on knowledge transfer technique. Each member of the offshore team is assigned to observe the work of one member of the onshore team. The onshore team member should explain what he is doing and why, the offshore team member should be taking notes and asking questions.

When the onshore team thinks that the offshore team is ready then the roles are reversed. The offshore team start doing the work for the first time and the onshore team will observe their work and offer encouragement or constructive criticism. Because they are being observed, if any major mistakes are made the onshore team can take over immediately if need be. So the risks of doing the job for the first time are reduced.

The advantage of this method is that it is practical and gives the offshore team their first taste of doing the work for themselves. It also has a natural way of dividing the work up between team members.

The disadvantage is that there is no guarantee that the whole scope of the activity is covered in this way. To compensate for this it is necessary for the transition manager to know the scope of the activity, to review the scope covered by the job shadowing and to find ways of including any missing subjects in the training.

Travel

Plan for the offshore team to travel to the onshore location at least once during the full transition. If there is an intention to do job shadowing then it is almost impossible to do this from a distance. You may also need to plan for members of the onshore team to travel offshore. Sending one member of the onshore team can provide a cost efficient follow-up to an onshore KT session with a team of people, it also gives the opportunity to see what it is like to work from offshore and whether any adjustments need to be made.

Meeting the onshore team helps build good relationships. Even though the onshore team is to be disbanded the two teams still need as much good will as possible during the transition for it to work smoothly.

In a complex full transition where every member of the offshore team needs to be part of the knowledge transfer then I would plan for each offshore team member to travel at some point. This is best implemented as a steady rhythm of small groups of people travelling for knowledge transfer, there is normally no need for the whole team to travel together.

It will also be necessary to plan for some members of the offshore team to meet the key user stakeholder as part of the KT, even if he is in a different country. He will be the one authorising the functional changes and approving the yearly budget so it is important to meet him and to understand how to work with him.

Certification

Many outsourcing vendors establish a product certification process during the transition period. This means that they draw up a number of written tests that they will use to ensure that the offshore team have achieved the necessary knowledge transfer. However, they don't just use the tests during the transition. Every time a new person joins the team they must complete the certification before they can take an active role within the team.

Regular incident or request follow up

The minimum requirement is that the offshore team should be able to take over all the normal daily activities of the onshore team, even if they are not yet ready to handle some of the more complicated activities that happen less often. To ensure that this is the case it is necessary to regularly review the work that comes in. For a production support activity look at the incidents that occurred and for a service based activity look at the requests that arrived.

I would recommend someone is assigned to reviewing the incidents or requests for the last 3 months to make sure that the team know what took place and that they know how to resolve the problems or deliver the necessary services. If they don't know then they need to ask the onshore team as soon as possible. Once the 3 months of history has been analysed, then each week's incidents or requests should be reviewed for the remainder of the transition period.

These reviews can identify whole areas of the activity that have been missed in the training, they can also help gauge how the transition to offshore is progressing.

Cutover

The goal is to achieve a gradual cut-over of responsibility between the onshore team and the offshore team. This should be a lower risk than a one time "big bang" complete cutover and it should be possible sooner thus allowing any issues with the knowledge transfer to be exposed as early as possible.

Typically the transition manager will look for ways to divide up the IT activity in order to provide a progressive ladder of responsibility to the offshore team until they own the complete activity.

For the example of an application production support activity then the application could be divided up into its constituent 4 major modules. In the beginning the offshore team take responsibility for all incidents affecting module 1 while the onshore team continues with the rest. A threshold may be set and any incident taking more than 2 hours to resolve must be handed back to the onshore team. Then at the end of each week the number of incidents raised for module 1 are compared with the number of incidents correctly resolved by the offshore team. Any incidents not resolved by the offshore team need to be analysed and as a result further knowledge transfer sessions may be needed.

When the offshore team is resolving all module 1 incidents themselves, without the help of the onshore team, then a decision will be taken for them to add module 2 to their scope. This process continues until all 4 modules are owned by the offshore team and then the transition is complete.

A similar approach can be taken with application development if the application can be easily divided into separate modules.

This concept can also be applied to software testing without needing to identify separate modules. The testing can start with a small number of key tests across the whole scope of the system. Then the number of tests are gradually expanded until the offshore team is executing all the documented tests for that application.

An alternative cut over approach for application development is to ask the offshore team to start with fixing bugs in the application before starting on maintenance and then finally to take on full development tasks. The area in which the bugs are fixed can be tracked and reviewed periodically to see if all areas of the application have been worked on by the offshore team or if there remain areas that need to be prioritised before moving on to the next stage of the cut over.

Staff retention

It is critical that the onshore staff remain throughout the transition period. This can be achieved by offering them alternative roles or by paying a successful transition bonus at the end.

Any transition bonuses need to be included in the business case costs for approval by senior management.

Transition quality assurance

The transition of a complete activity offshore is really a project in its own right. Therefore like any project there should be an independent review of the project before it starts, during the project (to make sure it is going in the right direction) and then again at the end to make sure it has achieved what it set out to do.

In a large organisation that has many activities to offshore then I would expect the offshore programme manager to have a dedicated team of offshore transition QA staff who would perform this role. In a smaller organisation I could envisage the transition managers reviewing each other's offshore transfer projects. Depending on the level of industrialisation of the company, it may also be able to use the KPIs of the service finally delivered to the end-users to help determine if the service contribution from offshore really matches what was being delivered previously when it was onshore.

This is not as easy as it sounds. I have witnessed a situation where a development team was transferred offshore, the end-user service KPIs implied that their service was as good as before, but the application support team believed that their work load had gone up and they were compensating for the non-availability of the offshore developers to answer user queries. Unfortunately they didn't have the KPIs for the support team to verify their claim but wished that they had.

Are you ready for offshore managed services?

Managed services versus extended teams

Extended teams rely on the onshore team to perform defined roles that have not been granted to the offshore team. There are advantages to a managed service but it is not possible to convert every extended team immediately into a managed service. Let's imagine that you have had an extended team for some years, the costs are increasing and now you are looking at how to control your costs by restructuring the offshore team as a managed service. This section explores the subtleties of this problem.

Company culture

Is the company culture supportive of managed service teams? If the global organisation has made it clear to everyone that managed service teams couldn't possibly work within their culture and that all offshore teams must be led from onshore then it will be difficult to launch offshore managed services.

Similarly, if all the onshore teams believe that they must have the last word on the recruitment of every member of the offshore team then it will be difficult to move to a managed service. However, if you find yourself in this situation then I suggest a slow reduction in onshore recruitment responsibility synchronised with an increase in offshore recruitment responsibility. Start with the most junior staff being selected only by the offshore team and then increase the level of recruitment responsibility over time until all the roles in the offshore team are selected offshore.

Another company culture issue can be with specialist roles such as business analysts, or architects. These roles may be needed within the managed service team but if your organisation's culture hasn't yet approved of these roles being in the offshore centre (even for extended teams) then it will be difficult to suddenly include them in a managed service team.

Service definition

Do you have the skills in your organisation to write a comprehensive Service Level Agreement (SLA), Operating Level Agreement (OLA) or software delivery contract through which the managed service could be measured and held accountable? Defining these documents is a key step towards being able to give the offshore team the responsibility it needs to operate autonomously. They need to know what to deliver, to what level of quality and by when.

This may be easier to draft for an operational activity such as application production support than it would be for a development activity but the principles are the same. This allows the team to be managed on outcomes and clear targets rather than through the tasks of the team members.

Team size

To be autonomous the team needs to be of a minimum size. Often people start extended teams with only 2 employees offshore. This is not enough for an autonomous managed service. The absolute minimum must be 4 people of which one of them would be the team leader.

If as the result of moving to an offshore managed service the onshore team will be disbanded, then this will also be described as a full transition. For this to work the number of resources needed offshore needs to be reviewed as you may need to recruit more people into the team before making this transformation.

Skills

If the team has been operating for some years then the major skills needed for the extended team should already be mastered by the offshore team.

Before transforming the offshore team to a managed service it is necessary to ensure that the offshore team has all the skills to achieve its new responsibilities. The minimum will be to make sure that they have the management skills necessary to run a managed service and that someone has been appointed as the team leader.

If this is also a full transition then there may also be technical or business analysis roles performed onshore that were never in the extended offshore team, these need to be identified, staff recruited and the knowledge transferred.

Methodologies

It may be a disadvantage to continue to follow the onshore methodology when the activity is fully transitioned offshore as a managed service. This is especially true if the onshore methodology was ad-hoc or unnecessarily light.

For a managed service it would be wise to employ a clear methodology and process that will support the transition offshore and keep a high level of quality after the transition. Investigate which methodologies you have available in the Captive Centre. Of the appropriate ones for this activity, see which ones the team members are already trained in to help make a decision on which one to use.

Documentation

Are the activity and the software product fully documented? Does the documentation consist of a knowledge portal, a Wiki, files on a shared drive or are they stored in a document management system? Does the offshore team have full access to this documentation and the rights to update the documents?

The complete knowledge will be required offshore. This may mean transferring document ownership to the offshore team, writing missing documents or using some other knowledge management tool to capture the knowledge.

Knowledge transfer challenge

It is likely that the transformation to a managed service is also a full transition of the onshore team to offshore. If this is the case then the knowledge needs to be transferred before the onshore team is disbanded and perhaps before the onshore team loses the focus or willingness to help. This is the final knowledge transfer challenge.

The onshore management has a big role to play in keeping the team motivated so that the transition can be successful. They must plan for the day the team is no longer needed and communicate what is going to happen. Their management should consider offering the team other opportunities onshore, or paying them a completion bonus and ensuring that they give good references.

When the experts have gone

After a full transition from onshore to offshore resulting in the creation of a managed service, no-one in the original team is left behind in the onshore location. When the activity was an extended team it would always have been possible to speak to one of the experts onshore if the offshore team got stuck.
The offshore managed service team must prepare its own staff for the departure of the onshore experts. They cannot all become experts overnight, so who can they turn to? Maybe there is someone already in the team who would relish becoming the expert in a particular area. If this is the case then this person should be given the responsibility and encouraged to become an expert. Perhaps there are experts in other offshore teams that could be identified now that could be called upon in times of emergency. If the onshore team is redeployed to other onshore roles then they too could act as a safety net if need be.

~~~

How does the vendor make it work?

Outsourcing vendor companies are successful

The biggest IT service companies with a large offshoring presence are very successful. Many of the largest companies of this type were started in India and are still Indian companies; e.g. Infosys, Tata Consultancy Services and Wipro to name just a few. They now have offices globally and many have made their early employees dollar millionaires.

Their objectives are not the same

We must remember that their business is selling IT services. Many people are looking at offshoring from the viewpoint within the IT department of a Major Corporation. The corporation's business is not IT, the IT department simply provides the IT services needed to support the real business in which the organisation makes its money.

Offshore IT service companies are very innovative. They have worked on every aspect of their business model to make as much money as possible while delivering what the client wants. Where the corporate IT department sees software products that would be difficult for them to offshore, the outsourcing vendor sees a money making opportunity. Where corporate IT sees a lack of resources for a particular technology the outsourcing vendor sees another business opportunity.

Talent attraction: Brand

In developing countries these ultra-successful offshoring companies receive good press and are household names. They are very attractive to local people who want a career in IT because they are dedicated IT companies. They have strong brands that they continue to build and leverage as much as possible.

A corporate global organisation may have a strong brand in its own country but maybe unheard of in a major offshore location. Those that are in the same line of business as the corporation may have heard of it, but the IT people in the offshore market may only know about IT companies and therefore the brand is not known to them.

Talent attraction: Career path

All the big offshoring companies have well developed career paths for their employees. For example, they are able to say with certainty that if a graduate developer achieves specific goals that within 5 years he can be promoted to project manager.
This may seem rather rigid but in practice it means that the employees know exactly what they need to do to achieve the next level in their career. Their path is clearly defined until they reach very senior roles.

Talent attraction: Early career growth

Within the offshore vendor organisation the rungs on the career path ladder are very close together at the beginning. Therefore a graduate entrant who has worked for 1 year will already have a different title to a new graduate entrant and he feels that he is making progress.

Financial rewards are linked to the formal career path. So climbing the ladder provides not only social recognition but also financial rewards.

Talent attraction: Overseas opportunities

Many people join large offshoring companies because they want the opportunity to work overseas. Despite their being a monetary advantage to the client by the outsourcing company doing as much work offshore as possible, it is still necessary to send people onshore. They will travel to prepare for offshore transition, for staff augmentation or to work directly with the users.

While these people are stationed onshore they will be paid close to western amounts. This is paid through a number of different overseas allowances. It is normal practice for staff being sent overseas to save as much of their overseas allowances as possible. The savings obtained from a 3 year placement in an expensive location such as New York could really set someone up financially for their return to their developing country.

Once overseas the employee may also make his own plan to stay there, thus using this temporary overseas assignment as a stepping stone to a new life in the western world.

Therefore you can see that the lure of overseas opportunities can be a real motivator to join the outsourcing vendor or to commit to staying with them.

Graduate Recruitment

The large offshore companies recruit more graduates than any other type of candidate. They like to recruit fresh graduates and mould them to become company men.

To achieve this they often start very early. They will target specific universities and influence the subjects to be taught to students during their undergraduate IT studies. This aims to ensure that they will be of value in the IT market at the time they graduate and hence a good fit to be recruited into the vendor company.

Similarly they will start visiting universities to speak to students long before they graduate. This helps build their brand as well as directly influencing graduates about their future direction.

As graduation approaches the offshore companies will interview candidates in huge numbers across thousands of universities before making offers. For those that accept the offers and join the outsourcing vendors they will enter into their graduate training programmes. All graduates are trained before they are assigned to their first activity.

Even when they have started on their first commercial activity they will not be forgotten. They are monitored and regular feedback is given. Every year they will receive more training to increase their usefulness to the company and to help them climb the ladder.

Senior recruitment and professional hires

In addition to graduates, offshoring companies also hire experienced professionals. These maybe recruited from end user organisations (offshore or local) or they could come from their offshoring competitors.

They will all be evaluated and placed on the company's career path. As a result they will also receive additional training every year.

Selection criteria: Languages

Global corporations with international clients normally insist that their offshore IT staff speak a good standard of English. An offshore IT services company will be happy to recruit someone who has good technical skills, who can speak the local language, but cannot communicate very well in English. They may deploy this person in a team where someone else can do all the English speaking or they may keep this person to work on local IT activities where it is not necessary to speak English to such a high standard.

In other words, Captive Centres may be missing out on good technical staff by insisting on such a high standard of English.

Selection criteria: Personal Presentation

An offshore IT company may be prepared to overlook the way someone dresses, or the way they have their hair if they think that the person either has great technical skills or that the person can be educated in how the company expects the person to look. I was told of a case where a man came for interview wearing bright nail varnish and a flowery shirt. He would normally have been rejected by this company as they knew someone looking like this would cause friction with the onshore client but they could tell that he had good skills so they offered him the ultimatum that if he wanted the job he had to dress the part and then come back to continue the interview. He changed his appearance, joined the company and was a real asset to the organisation.

Selection criteria: Long term technical staff

Outsourcing vendors don't offer only one career path to their staff. Becoming a manager is not the only route. This is important because they need experts in multiple areas. In particular they look after people who want to remain technical.

In my experience it is rarely the case that multi-national companies, whose business is not IT, offer equivalent rewards to IT technical staff as they do to those IT staff who want to become managers or join the business side.

All IT organisations, IT vendors and IT departments need people with very good technical skills. If they don't demonstrate that they value technical skills throughout someone's career over the long term then they will stay with IT service companies that do value them.

Salaries

Outsourcing vendors do not pay as well as Captive Centres. For a fresh graduate the training scheme, brand and career path offered by an IT offshore company compensates for the difference in salary.

As staff become more senior the gap grows between the salary paid by the vendor and the salary paid by the Captive Centre for the same role. At this point the benefits of staying with the vendor may well seem outweighed by the opportunity to get a large salary increase.

Travel costs

IT outsourcing vendor companies need to remain competitive and this requires minimising their travel costs. Therefore all staff will fly economy class and everyone will stay in economy hotels or company apartments. Interestingly, I have never met anyone who is bitter about this and so, I believe, it has been accepted as being part of the business model.

Captive Centres would like to minimise their costs but they are often constrained by the global rules of their organisation. As a result their travel costs are much higher.

This is a significant difference when problems occur between onshore and offshore. Often problems can only be resolved quickly by getting key staff onshore as fast as possible. If the travel is inexpensive then it is likely to be approved and the problem then gets solved quickly, otherwise having a debate about travel costs during an already difficult time doesn't help anyone.

Equipment costs

IT vendors will minimise their PC, server and network costs by using economy single screen models. In comparison the Captive Centre is influenced by what happens onshore and may well offer people multiple high-end PCs with multiple screens, lots of server storage space, their own laptop and tablet computer.
It is in the culture of the vendor to avoid these costs and to supply only the minimum needed to get the job done.

Premises costs

In the same location the outsourcing vendor will probably have marginally lower premises costs per seat than the Captive Centre. The level of finish of the premises may well be similar but the amount of desk space per person will probably be less.

The biggest difference in premises cost will be that the vendor is prepared to build offices in cheaper parts of the town or cheaper parts of the country. They will then be very selective about which activities take place in the more expensive offices and thus the overall cost of premises will be reduced.

Staff availability on the Bench

Offshore vendors keep staff on what is known as "the bench". This gets its name from the bench of players waiting to be called onto the pitch in a ball game. The outsourcing vendor has a strategy to never allocate 100% of their staff to client activities. Instead they will have a fixed minimum percentage of people waiting for new activities to be launched, this is their bench.
At any one time the bench will consist of people with different technical and business skills. If a new business opportunity arises then these people on the bench can be deployed immediately to start work. Or alternatively they could be used to back fill for people on existing activities who are a better fit for the new client activity.

People on the bench are still kept busy. In practice they maybe on a training programme or working on internal company (not client) activities from which they can be interrupted. No-one wants to be on the bench for long because one of the criteria for their yearly evaluation will be how many billable days they spent on client facing activities.

Staff Rotation

To actively manage staff along their chosen career path it is necessary to move staff to new roles that meet their personal development criteria.

When a new client activity starts there may be some agreement with the staff member to not change roles for the first 12 months, but after that it is likely that as soon as a role appears that meets his development needs that he will be transferred. This is most frustrating for clients but it is a strong retention factor for vendor companies.

Managed services and body shopping

As mentioned in the section on offshore models, outsourcing vendor organisations do not like doing body shopping. Their preference is to undertake all activities as a managed service. The revenue from body shopping is limited to the day rates of the people working for the client. The client has to interview and accept each and every person before allowing them on site. This is a big restriction on the number of people that can be deployed and hence a restriction on total revenue.

Also the body shopped staff have to work as if they were part of the client's organisation. So they don't have access either to the time saving devices that have been built by the vendor (e.g. templates and tools) nor do they have easy access to the experts in the vendor organisation.

During this time the vendor will see how the client delivers IT services. The outsourcing vendor may not get a good impression and this could convince him that he can undercut your costs and still make money. This will spur him on to pushing you to start a managed service with his organisation.

If the vendor can convince the client to allow them to deliver a managed service then they can make use of all the advantages just listed, plus they can follow the vendor's tried and tested delivery process and best of all use staff that may never have been accepted by the client. On the other hand, by accepting to deliver a managed service the outsourcing vendor takes the complete delivery risk and must deliver if he is ever to work with this client in the future.

Most outsourcing vendors are completely confident of their model and know that they can make more money from managed services. As a result of this, even if the vendor agrees to a temporary body shopping arrangement you can be sure that the relationship manager will soon be back to convince you to move the activity to a managed service.

Everything is a process

The big and successful offshore vendors don't leave anything to chance. They certainly don't let managers decide their own direction in isolation and wait to see if they succeed or not. Everything at the vendor will be scripted and defined in a process. This will range from simple actions such as organising training to complex project delivery.

The sum knowledge of the outsourcing vendor's successes, as well as their knowledge of industry best practices, will be built into these processes so that their successes are repeated.

Defined methodologies

The vendor will have clearly written methodologies for all major IT activities. For instance, a defined software development methodology.

All staff will be trained in the methodology and they will have to submit evidence that they are using it as instructed.

Experts involved at key points

The processes that they follow allows junior staff to make progress on IT activities on their own. At regular intervals what they have done will get reviewed by experts on the vendors staff. Therefore they will get the input they need from the experts without needing to have experts assigned to their team full time.

These people could be experts in business knowledge, processes, technology, architects, testing or any domain area that would be needed to make the delivery a success.

This allows for a greater use of the staff available as the number of experts in any organisation is always limited. Also it reduces the risk of following the wrong path for an extended period because these reviews are mandatory and they happen for all activities.

Business knowledge

Offshore vendors cannot rival end user IT departments for business knowledge. The in-house IT team has near unlimited access to the people who are doing the business every day. Also through recruitment of staff from their competitors' IT departments they will have gained business knowledge from the wider market too.

This is the biggest advantage that in-house IT teams have over IT vendors. The vendor may be better at IT but it will be a long time before they have more business knowledge. IT vendors know this and as a result they are taking steps to reduce the gap.

One approach is that the outsourcing vendors have hired experts directly from end-user IT organisations, both onshore and offshore. We can only assume that they have had to pay them competitively and therefore they must be real anomalies in their pay structure.

A longer term approach has been for vendors to build shrink wrapped line of business applications that can be sold to end user organisations where traditionally they would have developed their own. Initially they will not have had the business knowledge to compete with the in-house systems of tier-1 organisations. So they will start by working in partnership with lower tier organisations to build a product. These early adopters will partner with the vendor gaining lower IT costs and in turn bringing their business knowledge with them thus enriching the business knowledge of the vendor. Then the vendor will start selling to tier-3 and tier-2 end user organisations. The lower tier organisations will have small IT budgets and will quickly see the business case for using a good package product that has been implemented by their competitors. Their IT budget is not large enough to give them a real technology advantage. Eventually the vendor will have a product that is attractive to tier-1 end user organisations.

This is an ongoing process. As the vendor deploys his package product to more and more end user organisations his business knowledge will grow and so will his market penetration and revenues.

~~~

Successful enterprise offshore planning

Offshore Simulation

If the teams and team managers have had no experience of offshoring then they may benefit from starting with an offshore simulation exercise. The goal is to create the context of offshore working with an existing team in order to learn about the effects of working remotely and in a different time zone.

For the simulation it is necessary to identify an existing IT team and ask them to work from another location temporarily. This could be another office of the company, someone's home or a hotel room through a secure VPN connection. The team would be instructed to work the hours of the chosen country for offshoring. It is only the offshore location that is simulated, the team needs to continue with its real work for the exercise to be representative of the work offshore. The simulation needs to last until there is proof that they can work in this way, or that they have identified issues that once resolved would allow them to work.

This exercise can quickly raise confidence amongst the teams that remote working in a different time-zone is possible. The simulation may highlight some areas where problems may arise, such as a lack of collaboration tools. This can also be seen to be positive by the teams as they now know what the problems are and can focus on resolving them.

Offshore Pilot

If an organisation has never offshored activities in anyway, and the senior IT management hasn't had this experience outside the organisation, then a good way for an organisation to start offshoring is with a small pilot activity. This can transform the organisation's theoretical understanding of offshoring into a practical understanding with knowledge that can then be applied to the whole offshore programme.

Unless the organisation already has offices available in an offshore location, then it is most likely that the pilot offshoring activity will have to be with an outsourcing vendor. In this way a pilot can be started without finding premises or recruiting staff. Although this will give an experience of outsourcing, many of the lessons learnt will also be applicable to in-house offshoring.

The pilot must be defined with clear goals. A real service or real software delivery needs to be achieved by the pilot. It is not enough of a goal to have a good learning experience. The outsourcing vendor can be selected based on a check list of criteria and a meeting with two or three potential companies. Regardless of how well the pilot goes with the chosen vendor, be prepared to change vendors when the enterprise offshoring programme begins. At this stage the requirements of the service provider will be more complete and an in-depth study of more vendors will need to take place.

Discovery

After launching a pilot the onshore enterprise will have a good idea on whether it wants to go ahead with offshoring and what the goals of that offshoring will be. The most efficient approach is to then develop an offshoring plan for the whole enterprise rather than executing further pilots. In this way it is possible to plan the office requirements and the resource requirements to ensure that you have them at the time you need them.

The next step at this stage is to conduct what is called a "discovery" exercise. This is where an inventory is made of all the IT activities of the enterprise across all the countries within scope of the potential offshoring. The organisation may well have project lists and headcount data already, but it is unlikely to have a complete list of which technologies are used by which products, the hours of operation, the languages needed or the level of maturity of each product team.

It is essential that nothing is left out as there may be synergies between product areas that would otherwise be missed. For example, two teams using the same package product could be merged and offshored if the analysis identifies this possibility in the beginning. The discovery phase can either be conducted in-house, by a consulting firm or by an outsourcing vendor. Of course there is a risk of conflict of interest here as the outside parties will want to win more business, this has to be managed.

At the end of the discovery phase it should be easy to see some immediate offshoring opportunities, some areas that need more analysis and some areas that are unlikely to be ready for offshoring until later phases.

Enterprise strategy: Full service or specific activities

What will be the offshoring target and how can it be achieved in stages?

Will all of the following be included in the target scope?
- Application development
- Application maintenance
- Application testing
- Application production support
- IT remote infrastructure support

If all of these are to be offshored to the same location then this will be a "full service" offshoring and there will be efficiency gains achieved by collocating the teams.

Enterprise strategy: Business Operations and IT together?

Before finalising the IT enterprise offshoring plan it would be wise to talk to other departments to see if they are planning their own offshoring, even if it is for some years ahead.

If there is a plan to move a business operations team offshore then it means that the end users of one of the IT applications will move offshore and a combined offshore plan could locate IT and end-users in the same location therefore yielding further efficiencies. It is not necessary to convince another department to achieve a complete offshoring of their activity, but it would be useful to know if there is an opportunity for synergies to occur. Having end users in the same location can greatly increase the business knowledge of the IT team and this is the most precious resource there is when the offshore team has never worked directly with the users before.

Enterprise strategy: Global Sourcing

The combination of onshore, near shore and offshore locations that an enterprise chooses for service delivery would define their Global Sourcing Strategy. Such a strategy is equally relevant to those who intend to outsource their activities or to offshore them in-house.

The discovery exercise will help the enterprise to know where the existing IT activities are across the world, their hours of operation and which local languages work needs to be conducted in. Work can then begin to define the Global Sourcing Strategy by deciding which countries to keep activities in, which countries to offshore to and what their hours of operation will be. The strategy team can make use of the models for centralisation, follow the sun and shared utilities to reduce the number of IT locations and hence to simplify the offshoring.

The strategy team can choose to take advantage of the differences between offshoring countries, or between near shore and offshore locations to design the global sourcing model. Although, to keep it cost effective it is necessary to ensure that there will be enough volume of work to supply all the locations chosen in the strategy. There will always be a trade-off between the economies of scale achievable by using one single offshoring centre compared with the flexibility of using multiple centres in different time zones. Of course it is possible that the hours of operation, technical skills, and business knowledge or language skills may dictate that more than one location will be needed. With the locations identified then the next step is to decide for each location whether services will be delivered from an in-house captive centre or by an outsourcing vendor.

For example, imagine this global sourcing strategy for a retail confectionary sales corporation that has its headquarters in Brussels, Belgium. They may have a real-time payment gateway that is supported by an IT services company in Belgium (therefore an onshore local delivery). Their e-commerce site is supported in Poland (near shore) by an outsourcing vendor with French language skills, and the team that develops this site is in their Captive Centre in India (offshore).

Identifying activities to offshore

Having completed the Discovery exercise the enterprise will now have a complete inventory of all its IT activities globally. The next stage is deciding which activities to offshore.

First it is necessary to take in to account whether specific targets have already been set. A target comes from senior management and can take many forms.

Here are some examples.
- A dollar amount in cost savings.
- IT headcount offshore ratio.
- A dollar amount of IT offshored.
- Onshore geographic targets.

If specific targets have been issued like this then whether easy offshoring candidate activities are found or not, the analysis and planning will have to continue until the target is reached.

Never underestimate how this level of management pressure can open doors and make people get with the programme. Once managers realise their job is on the line then I have personally seen activities successfully offshored that 5 years before were deemed completely impossible.

Assuming the enterprise has a free hand to approach this subject scientifically, I propose the following minimum set of criteria is used to determine whether each and every IT activity can be offshored. The unit of analysis will be the complete team of people that do the job today, therefore not by task (too small) or by department (too large).

- Headcount
- Technology
- Business Knowledge
- Activity stability
- Process
- Documentation
- Team maturity
- Proximity
- Motivation
- Model
- Newness

Headcount: There must be enough budget to create at least 4 roles offshore where one will be the team leader, if it is less than this then see if it can be combined with another activity and assess again.

Technology: Are the core technologies used readily available in the offshore location? If not then would the lead time to learning the technology be acceptable?

Business Knowledge: How much business knowledge is required and in what areas? Can this knowledge easily be found offshore? What would the lead time be to transfer this knowledge?

Activity stability: How stable is the activity? If it is in the middle of a major change or is regularly failing in production then it might be better to wait.

Process: Does the activity follow any identifiable methodology or process? Mature process driven activities are easier to offshore.

Documentation: Is the documentation available and up to date? Good documentation reduces the offshore lead time and the transition risks.

Team maturity: How mature is the current team? Do the team have the knowledge needed to assist with the transfer?

Proximity: Are there any geographic constraints such as needing to be close to another team or end users? Can this problem be overcome?

Motivation: Is the current team showing interest in the offshoring? This can be a key piece of information in identifying the early quick wins. People who want to make it a success will see less barriers.

Model: What model of offshoring is being proposed and therefore what will be the onshore and offshore headcount after the transition?

Newness: Is there already something like this offshore? Is there an existing team that could be expanded to include this extra scope?

Note that in the selection criteria I have not aimed to categorise activities by client facing, back office, or uses new technologies. These are often talked about but from experience I believe this is an oversimplification of the problem. I have seen client facing activities offshored just as well as back room and admin activities. New technologies are certainly not a barrier to offshoring as the younger offshoring staff will have started straight out of school with these.

Governance for offshore programme go/no-go

The enterprise needs to make a decision officially as to whether it is going to pursue offshoring or not. Even if the CEO has set clear offshore targets as mentioned in the earlier section, it will still be necessary to get the major stake holders together to agree how this is going to work.

I would envisage a kick-off steering committee with the major stakeholders in the global IT department and their boss. The offshore plan for the coming year should be presented together with the long term goals. If the offshore target is well known for more than a year ahead then the planning for those years should also be presented.

Then a business case argument should be put forward for executing this plan. This would include the savings to be achieved, how the savings will be achieved, the risks, who will be affected, who will take responsibility and how the ongoing governance will work. Any major redundancy programmes, major infrastructure spending or legal issues need to be specifically highlighted.

Success in this meeting must equate to an unambiguous agreement to launch the offshoring programme.

Governance for offshore activity transition go/no-go

Even though the senior management will have agreed the offshoring plan for the year, it will still be necessary to agree the go/no-go transition of each and every activity. This is because the purpose of the offshore programme go/no-go would have been a high level agreement for the programme as a whole, there would not have been time to go into the details of hundreds of offshoring transition projects.

On-going activity transition governance

The same people that met for the transition go/no-go should meet again each month to review the progress of the transition. The progress will be measured against the transition plan that was presented and any investment amounts that were agreed.

The invitees to each activity transition go/no-go meeting will be the major stakeholders of the IT activity to be offshored together with the offshore programme manager. The IT manager of the activity to be offshored should present the business case for offshoring this activity and a clear plan with milestones and dates for the transition. The business case should include the following elements.

Savings: The amount of savings that can be achieved. An explanation of how these savings will be achieved. The amount that needs to be invested to achieve the savings. When the savings would be realised.

Risks: An explanation of the risks including a list of the principal transition risks and the execution risks.

Planning: A high level plan with milestones.

People: A list of the people whose employment or temporary engagement will be affected by this transition. In particular, state who will be at risk of redundancy.

Extension: Whether this transition offshore is an extension to an existing activity that is already offshore or whether it is something new.

Back-out plan: How the offshoring could be undone if necessary. The key elements of the plan to transition the activity back onshore to demonstrate that it is feasible.

Governance: Name who will take responsibility for the transition and how the ongoing governance will work after the initial transition.

Monitoring: Define the KPIs that can be used to track the progress of the transition activity and its success post transition. For this particular transition any staff redundancies, major infrastructure spending or legal issues need to be specifically highlighted.

~~~

Defining the Captive Centre strategy

Choosing the Captive Centre location

There are many countries that offer IT offshoring and near shoring.

The number one IT offshoring country is India. At the time of writing, China and Malaysia were the second and third largest (source AT Kearney GSLI 2014). There has been a recent rise in the interest for near shoring possibilities too. The locations that have grown their near shore offerings in the last few years include Mexico, Indonesia, Egypt, Mediterranean Europe and Eastern Europe.

The choice of country needs to fit well with your enterprise strategy. For example, if you are expanding in Europe then it may make sense to have a near shore centre in Eastern Europe.

When selecting a location the following points need to be considered:
- IT staff costs
- IT skills availability
- Languages spoken
- IT outsourcing vendors present
- Captive Centres present
- Time zone of operation
- Local tax and customs regimes
- Legal environment
- Government incentives
- Economic stability
- Political stability
- Technical infrastructure
- Other country risk

The availability of IT skills needs to be looked at in detail. You need to consider what it would be like to recruit staff or engage vendor staff in that country. For instance, a country may have good IT skills for maintenance of applications but very few people who could build a big application. Alternatively, there may be a good number of senior staff available but not enough new graduates being produced each year which would imply that costs will increase.

Global offshoring centres, such as India, tend to specialise in English language skills. Smaller offshoring countries may offer more languages but there will be a trade off with the IT skills that they have available.

Look to see who else is present in the country that you have shortlisted. If large outsourcing vendors or large Captive Centres are already established then it is a good indicator that they see long term value in being in this country. It could also mean that they have established a good pool of senior staff that may be open to transferring to your organisation.

Relative to where your home location is, the normal work day in each country may overlap more or less with your work day. You may want it to overlap as much as possible so that the opportunities to work together are maximised, or you may prefer that the offshore location does most of its work in the early morning so that everything is finished by the time your team comes in. Outside these normal working hours, depending on the country, it may be possible to get people to work shifts so that they are available at different times. This needs to be considered country by country.

If you create your own Captive Centre then at some point it will end up paying local corporation taxes. Therefore the corporate tax regime for the countries you are considering need to be investigated. Corporation tax and customs duties vary greatly between different countries. From a management accounting point of view you may have projected attractive cost savings through offshoring, but once the tax situation is included then a financial accountant may show you a serious reduction in your estimated savings. In this respect, China and Mexico may offer long term tax advantages compared to India.

The legal environment including the implementation of copyright and data privacy laws is not the same in all countries. In some countries copyright laws do not exist or are ignored, leading to large scale piracy of intellectual property. Data privacy laws have not yet been implemented in every country. This means that you have to be sure that the work you want to offshore to these countries is legally acceptable. There are regulated activities that will not be permitted in countries that do not have data privacy laws. Alternatively, you may have little choice in which country to use and as a result you would need to use strict procedures and practices to compensate for the legal system and then to apply to the regulator for an exemption.

Governments may offer incentives to create a captive centre in their country. This may be achieved geographically through the creation of special economic zones in selected parts of the country, or by offering schemes that a company can become part of if it meets certain criteria. An example of a specific scheme is the Software Technology Parks of India (STPI) programme whereby a physical office can be declared a custom bonded premises, pay no corporation taxes for the first few years and be exempt from import taxes on all equipment purchased. Typically all of these government schemes reward their participants in terms of tax breaks of one kind or another, the most frequent being lower corporate taxes for a specific number of years. These incentives can really offer significant cost savings.

There may be economic instability in the country you have selected. This could lead to wild swings in foreign exchange rates, or high salary inflation. As a result your offshore services may cost more than you had planned.

Political instability can manifest itself in unexpected changes in the laws of the country. For instance, repatriation of profits to the parent company could suddenly be taxed at 99%. Alternatively, political risk could lead to riots or strikes which would deny access to offices on work days.

The availability and the quality of technical infrastructure needs to be understood before making any high level cost estimates of offshoring to a particular country. Regular outages in the electricity supply can require the implementation of expensive electricity generators for a Captive Centre. Network infrastructure must be available throughout the working day, so check that the infrastructure is reliable and that there are alternative routes for network traffic out of the country if the primary route should fail. Enquire about the cost of leased lines for WAN connections out of the country, some low cost offshoring locations have surprisingly expensive network connections.

Other types of country risk could include the susceptibility to natural phenomena such as earthquakes, cyclones or monsoons (leading to floods). The imminent risk of these phenomena may leave people unable to attend the office, or even unable to leave the office. If the situation actually occurs then it could lead to a long period of time in which the office is no longer operational. Once the country has been decided then the location within the country needs to be selected. Choosing the right city in a large country requires a re-assessment of the same criteria presented for countries. This is particularly true in India where there is a wide difference between the IT skills available in different established offshoring areas (e.g. Gujarat compared to Bangalore).

By way of example let us consider a city that is new to offshoring compared to a long established one. It could be an advantage to select the newer location due to the lower staff costs or a disadvantage due to the lack of experienced staff.

Dual site

You may end up with multiple offices to achieve your offshoring goals, but the concept of a dual site is much more than having multiple offices and it requires more planning. Organisations that conduct time critical activities in countries where there is a risk of their offices not being available, may want to consider a dual site strategy in order to reduce their operational risks.

In this case two offices are established to implement the exact same type of work at the same time. This is not a follow the sun implementation, both offices are open at the exact same times. The two offices need to be far enough apart that the reason for the non-availability of one office would not impact the second office, typically this means that they would be hundreds of miles apart in the same country or located in separate countries. If one of the offices becomes unavailable for business then the other office can take over the complete workload. Therefore both offices must have enough spare capacity to be able to take on this extra workload.

This type of Dual Site strategy is implemented for critical activities such as payment processing, where no delays can be accepted and penalties will apply if deadlines are not adhered to. Of course this strategy is expensive because it requires the redundancy of two fully fitted offices with enough spare staff capacity to take on extra work.

Captive centre as a profit centre or a cost centre

It needs to be decided early on whether a captive centre will recharge only its costs back to its internal clients (therefore a cost centre) or whether it will sell its services to its internal clients for a profit (therefore a profit centre).

This seemingly small difference in strategy can have huge implications on the success or failure of the offshoring initiative and therefore on the cost savings that can be achieved.

The following points need to be considered:
- Client billing
- Self-funding
- Cost mark-up
- Fixed price contracts
- Investment strategy
- Late arrival attractiveness
- Early adopter attractiveness
- Market competition

If the Captive Centre is a profit centre then it can behave like an external outsourcing company. It can set its own prices for work, guarantee fixed price contracts and use its reserves to pay for its own investment.

In the cost centre model the Captive Centre is obliged to charge back every last penny of its activities, and no more, to the correct internal clients. A cost centre captive can only estimate the cost of a project or service, it cannot guarantee the price. Any undershoot or overshoot on costs must be billed to the client.

Therefore the profit centre has a lot of flexibility because it can choose how to raise capital (by setting its prices) and then can use any surplus funds to pay for underperforming fixed price projects or to invest in new technologies that might help it in the future.

Any additional investment a cost centre offshore organisation wants to make has to be approved by the parent organisation and fully recharged to them. If they are too far away to know whether this is a good use of their funds then this can create a difficult situation.

There may be a concern amongst those who first use the profit centre captive that they are being charged to generate profits that will then be used to subsidise other internal businesses that want to offshore. They may not see this as being very fair.

In the cost centre model all investment is made directly by the parent organisation, therefore right from the beginning all target business lines will be asked to contribute to the expansion of the Captive Centre. Thus a business line can join later on knowing that its part of the investment has already been paid and it is not subsidising anyone else. In comparison, late comers to the profit centre offshore organisation may be attracted by the thought that the offshore centre has already been subsidised by the profits gained from the activities of other business lines.

Normally the use of a cost centre captive is mandated by the parent organisation so everyone must use it as their primary offshoring choice. The profit centre captive normally has no such mandate, so if a business line finds the costs too high or the quality of work poor then it is free to use 3rd party outsourcing centres. This could be a good thing because it keeps the offshore centre competitive, but as it is difficult to bring work back in-house once it has been outsourced then it is likely to lead to a fragmentation of the offshoring strategy and a loss of confidence and revenue for the captive centre.

I have observed a profit centre Captive in a very difficult situation that would be unlikely to arise for a management mandated cost centre captive. Senior management wanted the profit centre captive to succeed but they had to let market forces rule as that was implicit in choosing a profit centre model.

The profit centre Captive was competing head-on with major outsourcing companies for small internal IT projects. The external companies were able to use their professional sales force and greater local presence in the onshore location to win business. It didn't help that the onshore internal project managers only had to report the man years quoted by the internal and external suppliers in order to justify who got the business. So even when the profit centre Captive was cheaper than the external companies, if the man/years quoted was more than that quoted by one of the outsourcing vendors then the contract would be signed with the external party. Unfortunately the internal project managers had no incentive to offshore their projects to the profit centre Captive and it couldn't be mandated. This was clearly not a good situation and was putting the offshore strategy at risk.

The resolution was for the profit centre Captive to enter into a formal agreement with the onshore management to guarantee the price of a pre-agreed block of offshore man/years. This pool of pre-purchased resources was then made the primary supplier to the project managers. The size of the resource block and its price was negotiated each year, thus keeping the principle of market forces.

In summary, this strategic choice is so significant that it needs to be made by the highest management in the global organisation possible, after they have been fully informed by the major stakeholders.

Integration: Corporate Values

Often an organisation decides upon a set of core values that it believes defines the culture of the organisation as it is already or that it aspires to being. A global organisation will insist that these values are applied to all its offices and activities across the world. If you want the new Captive Centre to feel that it is part of the global organisation, and not just a vendor or supplier, then the parent company's corporate values need to be embraced and implemented locally. Different business lines within the global organisation may then add their own values to the core set of corporate values. In the same way the Captive Centre may choose to add some non-conflicting key values to those of the corporate core set.

Integration: Company Policies

The parent organisation will have a set of policies that it expects to be implemented in all its businesses and offices.
My personal view is that unlike the corporate values, the policies should be looked at very carefully before implementing them in the Captive Centre.

An example of this would be the high-level travel policy. If the parent organisation travel policy is for everyone to travel business class then implementing it in the captive might not be a good idea due to the high volume of flights needed and hence the increased cost it will incur compared to traveling economy. Remember that the offshore centre is in continual competition with external vendors. Market forces are always present even if the Captive Centre has been mandated by top management.

Integration: Company Procedures

These need to be looked at carefully. Some of the parent organisation procedures may work without changes in the offshore centre. If they are fit for purpose then they can be implemented, at the very least it will save writing a new procedure and at best it will help integration with the parent company.

Integration: HR Policies & Procedures

The real assets of the offshore activity are the people, not the buildings or the IT infrastructure. Therefore the Human Resources team, their policies and procedures are critical to the success of the Captive Centre. As a wholly owned subsidiary company of the parent organisation it will be mandatory to implement certain HR practices whereas others may be open to interpretation.

For instance, it will probably be mandatory to report headcount numbers, leavers and joiners to the parent HR department.

Training programmes will probably be at the discretion of the local HR team. This is good because the offshore centre will have specific training needs that will not be the same as those of the parent organisation.

Yearly, or twice yearly, career appraisals for all staff are normally mandatory in the parent organisation and will be just as useful in the offshore centre. The high level staff compensation policy will be dictated by the parent but the details of the implementation will be the responsibility of the offshore centre. This is critical because the compensation system needs to take into account the local IT market including major outsourcing vendors and competitor's offshore centres.

Recruitment Agency selection

If you decide to recruit permanent staff within the Captive Centre then you will need help in identifying those candidates. This is the purpose of an external recruitment agency. Some large Captive Centres do most of this work themselves with their own internal recruitment agency, but as their scope and volume of recruitment is large they still work with 3rd party recruitment agencies as well.

In a mature and organised market the selection of recruitment agencies through a Request for Proposal (RFP) procedure would be normal. Unfortunately, the recruitment markets in developing countries are rarely organised and therefore a different approach is used. Recruitment agencies are "tested" and the decision to continue with them is based purely on whether they found candidates, whether the candidates passed the interviews and if offers were made. This is a quantitative appraisal of how they have performed during their test period. Even when this trial period is complete, their performance is still monitored in terms of hard numbers.

This is a typical cycle for a recruitment agency relationship.

1. The current agents are not filling all the roles, so a new one is identified.
2. The new agency is asked to agree terms and conditions with the offshore centre and sign a supply contract with no guarantee of any future business. This is not a negotiation, the agency is told what the offshore centre is prepared to pay based on its knowledge of the market.

3. The agency is tested by asking it to find candidates for one open position (other agencies may also be searching for the same position).
4. If they don't make any progress then they are dropped. Or if they found a candidate they will join the preferred list.
5. All open positions are then communicated to all the agencies on the preferred list simultaneously, and they "compete" to fill the roles.
6. There will be a monthly review of each agency. If a new agency has not filled any roles in the last month then it will be dropped from the preferred list and will no longer receive instructions for open positions.
7. If the agency has been dropped but there is good reason to continue doing business with them then they may return to step 3 and test them again.

Captive Centre HR management

Decisions need to be taken jointly between the IT management and the HR management on the staffing strategy for the Captive Centre. Every year I would expect to set targets for the mix of permanent senior staff, permanent graduate entry staff, freelance staff and outsourced staff. These targets should be monitored by HR management and escalated if they are not being achieved.

A decision also needs to be taken on the ratio of "billable" staff (those who deliver services that are visible to the parent company) compared to "non-billable" staff who provide the management and support services needed for the Captive Centre. I would expect the ratio of HR management staff to IT staff to be higher in the Captive Centre than in the onshore location. The reasons for needing more people are that the captive centre will be recruiting far more people each year than the stable parent organisation, the staff in the captive centre will expect more career management from the HR team, attrition management will be needed and there will be more KPIs to produce.

The requirement for additional KPIs will be partly because the Captive Centre needs to be more transparent than the parent company and partly because the Captive Centre will need the KPIs in order to be more process driven. One of the HR KPIs that everyone will be interested to see will be the rate of attrition for captive centre permanent staff. There are many ways to calculate this and the final number will be different depending on the method used. My advice would be to choose a method that is the same as your nearest strategic competitor. Your competitor may be a particular vendor or another Captive Centre. This way at least your attrition figures will be comparable as long as the competitor follows the rules.

~~~

How to reduce Captive Centre long term costs

Regular benchmarking

Captive Centres need to be regularly benchmarked against external suppliers if they are to remain viable and able to withstand criticism from within the global organisation. However strong the mandate is from top management there will always be someone who believes that a particular outsourcing vendor could do the same job for less cost. This will be the first claim that the sales representative will make when he meets your top management.

To be prepared for this situation a benchmark comparison is necessary. This exercise will aim to match like for like activities and compare the unit cost. Some well understood activities can be compared in terms of volume, such as the number of accounts payable invoices processed, and therefore a comparison can be made on the cost per transaction. Other activities such as software development are harder to compare on volume and therefore will be compared on cost per person for the same type of software development activity. For software development this goes against the in-house teams as it is likely to have fewer but more expensive staff than the outsourcing vendor would have for the same activity. Of course a comparison has to be made somehow.

The Captive Centre doesn't have to beat the average vendor's costs to win the benchmark. It just needs a good like for like comparison and to be able to explain the cost differences. No doubt the Captive Centre has many attractions compared to the vendor, these need to be given an estimated monetary value to the parent company so that they can be offset against the cost disadvantages the benchmark has found.

For the benchmarking process to be independent and for it to have access to the data from competitor organisations it is necessary to use an external benchmarking service. Many IT and Management consultancies will offer this service.

In the following sections I will outline a few ideas to reduce long term costs and to become more competitive in the next benchmark.

Using permanent attrition

You may think that all staff attrition is bad news. No-one ever wants to lose the staff that they have invested in. Unfortunately, attrition is going to happen so you should aim to get some benefit from it. You may have IT activities that function perfectly well with junior staff. If there is no attrition then the junior staff will eventually become senior staff and as their salaries increase so the total staff cost will keep rising. Therefore in this situation attrition can be used as an advantage. The team manager can replace senior leavers with new junior staff and thus lower the average level within the team and keep the costs down.

Redeploying permanent resources

In a similar way to the previous example, if you have an activity where you need to keep the cost down then you can actively plan to redeploy the maturing staff to other areas where they are needed which allows you to replace them with more junior staff and thus to keep the costs down.

Transition from extended team to managed service

Extended teams are not the cheapest offshore team model. They are reliant on the onshore management (which has a cost) and there is a risk that they will be less productive than when they are totally responsible for the activity themselves. Furthermore, an extended team is likely to be staffed mainly with senior staff whereas a managed service will be a pyramid of seniority which also leads to lower staff costs.

Therefore extended team structures should be reviewed at least once per year to decide if they would be better structured as a managed service.

165.   Transition of activities to an outsourcing vendor
There may be situations where cost savings could be made by transferring an activity from the Captive Centre to a vendor's outsourcing centre.

For instance, if in-house staff are being used to build tools for the Captive Centre then you might make savings by redeploying these staff onto billable activities and transferring the tool development to an outsourcing vendor. Or you may have an IT activity that is completely stable offshore and you feel confident that now it is fully process driven that it doesn't justify having the senior staff working on it within the Captive Centre. So it can be transitioned to an outsourcing vendor.

Limit the number of expatriates

In the beginning it might be necessary to inject business knowledge, technical skills and management into the Captive Centre in order to achieve the early deliveries. This is often managed by expatriating some key senior staff from onshore. The downside of this is that expatriates are expensive and they don't provide a long term solution because their secondment is normally limited to 3 years. Be prepared to replace expatriates with local staff and therefore to achieve cost savings. If a developer is offshore for 3 years then that should be plenty of time to share his knowledge with local staff so that he is not replaced with another expatriate at the end of his term. Create an expatriate replacement plan, ensure that every expatriate features in this plan and keep it up to date.

Continuous process improvement and cost reduction

Establish KPIs for the organisation. Set thresholds for these KPIs. When they pass your defined thresholds then look at how the processes can be improved to keep the KPIs on track and therefore control the costs.

These KPIs should include:
- Billable staff utilization
- Bench staff numbers
- Labour pyramid (staff by seniority)
- Average time to hire new staff
- Attrition of permanent staff
- Ratio of staff overhead versus billable staff
- Invoice average time to payment
- Infrastructure KPIs
- IT delivery KPIs

Nurture a culture of continuous process improvement and cost control. Let staff know that each of them has a responsibility to improve on the processes that they use every day, they should not be waiting for permission or waiting for an independent team to audit their processes. Encourage people to communicate the process improvement and cost reduction successes they have achieved and ensure the best ones receive company wide recognition.

Alternatively, in a larger Captive Centre a small continuous improvement team can be created. These need to be experts in change management and coaching. Often these teams are also experts in LEAN or Six Sigma methodologies. They will work with all teams in the captive on a rotation basis to coach them through making continuous improvements and implementing cost reductions.

Target external certifications

Improvements can be made in the Captive Centre if everyone works together to reach a shared target. Enterprise level external certifications provide publicly recognisable targets for the captive to reach.

One such certification is CMMi. This is a global standard for process maturity measurement and appraisal. An example of its use would be to run an internal programme to lift the Captive Centre from CMMi level 2 to level 3. This would not only improve the processes in the organisation and reduce delivery risks, but it would also be an improvement that would be understood by industry experts who may be asked to appraise the captive centre.

Before embarking on an external certification path it is necessary to think about how tied the Captive Centre is to the parent organisation. If the Captive Centre alone is going to be appraised for an external certification then it needs a degree of autonomy from the parent organisation, otherwise the parent will also need to be appraised. For instance, if the Captive Centre is full of extended teams then it would be impossible to claim that the Captive Centre is responsible for its own processes end to end, by definition there is an external team manager onshore for each external team. On the other hand, if we took the example of a profit centre Captive housing only managed service teams then it would have complete autonomy to be appraised for its own processes. These are extreme examples, often the autonomy of a real Captive Centre lies somewhere in-between.

Invest in good communication tools that reduce the need to travel

Everyone wants to talk to their team members and users overseas. Make sure you have enough video conference rooms, that they are used and that the picture quality is sufficient. Instant messaging needs to be available to everyone onshore and offshore. The leading tools also allow multiple people to join the same conversation.

Use tools that provide online spaces that staff can customise for their own communication needs. Examples include Wiki sites and Microsoft SharePoint.

Selecting and managing the vendors

Outsourcing Vendor selection

If you have decided to use an outsourcing company to supply staff, to provide complete teams or even to engage in the transition of whole activities on your behalf then you are going to need to choose the right vendor company. How you do this will depend on which stage you are at in your offshoring programme and how big the stakes are.

If you are at the pilot stage, or the invoice amounts will be very small, then it might be enough to meet a few outsourcing vendors and get official quotes from them. However, if by selecting the vendor you would then be starting a long term partnership where the billing over the years would amount to several million dollars then I would strongly advise taking the approach I will outline in this section.

For large third party relationships you want to be able to prove to anyone that asks that a professional selection exercise has taken place and that there has been no opportunity for corruption or other non-professional behaviour. This requires running an RFP (Request for Proposal) selection process in the following manner.

Step 1. Identify likely candidate outsourcing vendors, they could be existing suppliers, companies you have met, referrals or new companies from your own research. There must be at least two of them and be prepared to add more even once the process has started.

Step 2. Speak to the companies on the list and tell them that you would like to include them in a selection exercise.

Step 3. Assemble a team of people and write the RFP. List all the questions to which you need to know the answers in order to make your selection. Get the input of your procurement department if you have one.

Step 4. Distribute the RFP to all your candidate outsourcing vendors and give them a specific timeframe to respond to the RFP and a clear mechanism by which to answer their questions.

Step 5. When you receive a question from anyone of the vendors then systematically send the reply to all the vendor candidates to give them an equal chance.

Step 6. When the RFP answers are received then review them with your RFP team and aim to eliminate those that don't meet the minimum criteria.

Step 7. Invite the remaining vendors to present their proposals in person, use this meeting to clarify any of their answers that were not clear.

Step 8. Rank the outsourcing vendors based on an agreed set of criteria and review again within the RFP team.

Step 9. Make the selection and announce it to the vendors.
The RFP needs to cover many subjects and is likely to run to many pages. The answers to some of the questions in the RFP will feed straight into the contract or statement of work so it is important to get them right at this stage.

Questions need to include the following subjects.
- Pricing
- Offshore Availability
- Onshore Availability
- Attrition levels
- Contract length
- Price review
- Languages
- Security
- Staff training
- Staff selection
- Technology

- Business Knowledge
- Specialisms
- Scope of services
- Contract management
- Continuous improvement
- Grievances
- Methodologies
- Examples
- Client References
- Vendor goals
- Financial strength
- Industry Partnerships

Pricing: What will the price be for time and materials? How is the pricing structured (e.g. by staff seniority or by technology)? What discounts are available (e.g. volume reductions on big staff engagements)?

Offshore availability: How many staff does the vendor have available by technology area or by domain? Are there limitations to this in practice that should be known? Does the supplier operate a bench?

Onshore availability: How many staff does the vendor have outside its home (offshore location)? Do they have any staff based in the onshore location? These could help onshore teams with analysis, problem solving and transition.

Attrition levels: How much attrition has there been for each of the last 5 years?

Contract length: What length of agreement must be entered into?
Price review: How long are the quoted prices valid for? Would there be a formal review or an automatic review with price increases?

Languages: Which spoken and written language competencies are possible from the vendor's offshore location?

Security: How will the vendor ensure that the work space is secure through physical and IT security? How will the vendor ensure the high availability of the ODC?

Staff training: What facilities does the supplier have for staff training? What is their policy for training staff? Is there a mandatory training period every year?

Staff selection: How does the supplier select its external recruits? What would the role of the client be in this selection? What happens if a particular one off role is required for the client? Technology: Which technologies does the supplier support? Are there any that he will not support?

Business Knowledge: What is the level of business knowledge within the supplier's organisation? Are there any specialist business knowledge skills relevant to the client that the vendor wants to highlight?

Specialisms: Does the supplier have any centres of excellence?

Scope of services: Does the supplier offer a full range of IT services (e.g. development, application support, application testing, maintenance and IT remote infrastructure management)?

Contract management: How will the high level engagement be managed? What governance will be put in place? How will results be measured?

Continuous improvement: What will the vendor do in order to continually improve the service?

Grievances: How would the client raise issues with the supplier?

Methodologies: Which methodologies does the supplier use? Does it make use of industry best practices? The scope of this subject is from analysis through to QA.

Examples: What examples can the vendor give of real activities he has conducted for real clients? Look at the size of the client activities he has performed, does it match the size you need? Client references: Which of the vendor's clients can be visited to provide a reference for the vendor?

Vendor goals: What are the stated goals of the company, what type of company do they aim to be? Are they aligned with your needs?

Financial strength: Does the vendor have a good financial standing and is likely to remain in business for the length of the contract?

Industry Partnerships: Does the supplier have official partnerships in place with major technology providers (e.g. Microsoft or Oracle)?

I suggest you attach your own weighting to each of these question categories so that you can quickly rate the answers and eliminate vendors that cannot meet your key criteria. With the question categories and the ratings derived from each vendor's answers you could build a matrix allowing you to easily compare the vendors.

Not everything in the RFP will be a question. It is also important to communicate as accurately as possible what you need the vendor to do over the coming years. It is not necessary to list your requirements project by project, but you will need to give a picture of the throughput and rhythm of work you are expecting. For example, if the vendor knows that he needs to provide 1000 people for the next two years and then ramp this down to 500 for the following 5 years then this will help him reduce the uncertainty of the engagement and hence reduce the cost of the engagement to you.

Master Services Agreement

If you intend to start a long term agreement with an outsourcing vendor then, following the selection of the vendor, you should enter into a Master Services Agreement (MSA). The MSA is an umbrella legal contract that defines the terms and conditions of the business that the two organisations will engage in. No IT work will start as the result of signing an MSA but the legal and commercial groundwork will have been laid for work to start.

There are parts of the MSA that will be the main responsibility of the company's lawyers (on both sides) and the procurement department, then there are other sections that start to define the IT services at a high level. You need to make sure that you are in complete agreement with the IT services section. For instance this may state the type of IT services to be provided, the countries of operation, offshore engagement models, invoicing models and could even include a schedule of T&M costs.

Statement of work

The real value of the MSA becomes apparent when you launch real work engagements with the outsourcing vendor. Instead of writing a complicated contract each time you want the vendor to do a piece of work, you simply issue a statement of work (SOW). This is a much lighter document than a full contract because it refers to the terms and conditions in the MSA and saves you renegotiating this part with the legal teams. In other words it is as though each statement of work automatically includes all the details of the MSA without needing to repeat them.

For example, the statement of work for a simple T&M engagement maybe as light as a list of the technical roles that you require, the number of headcount and the length of the engagement.

Even though these statements of work don't require legal experts to complete them, they can still trigger large invoices. Therefore it is critical that you have a suitable approval mechanism in place with a defined ladder of who can sign depending on the total cost.

Managing with long term objectives

The goal is to have the outsourcing vendor deliver the services that you want, on the dates proposed, with the agreed level of quality and all for a fair price. To achieve this you need to set up the engagement correctly with the vendor and then manage the vendor right the way through the delivery period until you get what you want or the relationship is terminated.

In most cases you would have chosen a vendor with the expectation that they will work with you as a long term partner so that you can entrust them with your long term activities (e.g. application production support for the entire life of an application). As a result of this you will want to resolve any differences when they arise rather than rushing to take legal action or transferring the business straight away to another supplier.

Managing T&M engagements

Unless any special arrangement has been agreed, the price of a T&M engagement will reflect the costs in the MSA or an alternative schedule that has been approved for all engagements with this vendor.

How you manage the vendor for a T&M engagement depends on what type of work you asked them to do. You may have asked them to provide a defined number of staff with a specified skill set. The vendor will first supply the CVs of the people he has chosen to work on this engagement that fit the criteria he received. Immediately you start the clock ticking and make a record of what happens. You get your staff to read the CVs and reject the ones that don't match the requirements, then you interview the remaining staff and you keep a record of the successes and failures.

The vendor may not like this because he has already chosen the staff for this engagement but you must ensure the quality of the staff right from the beginning. If it is taking time to complete the team in the statement of work then you will need to escalate this to the vendor through their relationship manager and share the records with them. It would be more difficult to make your case if you hadn't kept records.

If the your own staff are managing the vendor staff and are also responsible for the deliveries (e.g. a staff augmentation engagement) then you can measure the service provided by the vendor through the productivity of the staff he has provided you with. Even though you interviewed all the staff before they started, if at any later stage any vendor staff member is underperforming then you need to raise this to the vendor representative immediately. The vendor will ask for time for the resource to show his potential and perhaps propose he goes on a training course. Set a date for his next review and insist that the vendor exchanges him for a better resource if he doesn't shape up by the next review. Any knowledge transfer to a replacement person must be at the vendor's expense. Despite this confident approach you have to concede that you will not have an unambiguous metric for the vendor staff's productivity with the staff augmentation model so the evidence maybe called into question.

If the engagement is a managed service billed as T&M then you would not aim to manage the vendor through the quality of the staff unless their performance is truly terrible. Instead, as part of the managed service engagement you will have written the criteria for the success of the engagement and agreed it with the outsourcing vendor. At the first sign of not meeting this agreement you need to raise your concerns to the vendor.

Managing fixed price software delivery

This is very different to managing T&M. A software delivery engagement of any size will have a defined plan that will divide the activity into separate phases. Even though it is a fixed price engagement there may well have been an agreement to make stage payments once key milestones have been reached. If you consider that paying the invoice is the strongest bargaining tool available in this type of engagement then you will be managing the vendor milestone to milestone.

The price of this engagement will not have been defined by the MSA. Despite this, you need to know that a fair price is being quoted for the fixed price delivery. Even though the outsourcing vendor has been told that he is the preferred vendor, you will still ask another vendor (probably the runner up in the selection exercise) to bid for the same piece of work. Not only does this create some healthy price competition but it also allows you to see how much the two bids may diverge and hence whether either of them really understands what they have been asked to do.

I would also recommend that you make an internal high level estimate of the cost using your own teams, just to make sure that the bids you receive are realistic and that they are not both misunderstanding the requirements.

The definition of the deliveries to be achieved by this engagement with the vendor must be measurable. You will use these measurements to manage the vendor's performance and also to determine in advance whether you think that there is evidence that the project will succeed or that it will fail. Note that failure in this context doesn't just mean that the vendor will never make the delivery, it would also be a contractual failure to not deliver what you asked for with an acceptable level of quality by the date agreed.

You can measure the project's progress against the agreed key milestones. Each of the milestones has dates. You will be looking for both milestone dates that have not been met and delivery dates in the future that you think will not be achieved.

Most project delivery engagements will have a project risk register. Each of the risks will be identified and given a likelihood of occurrence as well as an impact rating. When real issues arise you can compare them to the risk log and see if the issues you are facing are in line with what was expected or whether there are too many and therefore the project is going out of control. This too is measurable.

When parts of the software are ready for testing, or reaching integration testing with other services or you have received the full delivery, then the Quality Assurance (QA) process will identify if there are defects. You can compare the number of defects and the rate at which they are being closed against the plan to see if you believe you will reach the next milestone on time. As an example, the vendor may show you that they are closing 20 bugs per day, but they are opening 22 new bug cases per day so they are not converging towards an acceptable delivery.

If any of the measurable items just listed indicates that there is a risk that the vendor will not reach the next project milestone by the agreed date then you must raise this immediately with the vendor relationship management.

To add to the complexity, it is possible that you need to change the software requirements during the project. This is officially called a change request. The impact of the change request may result in a new project plan being issued with modified milestone dates. If you accept the new plan then you must change the measurements to use the new milestone dates. Having received the change request the vendor may increase the fixed cost of the project. This may lead into another negotiation.

The outcome of a failure to meet the key milestones should be included in the statement of work with the vendor. The contract could include cash penalties or senior level escalations for non-compliance with key milestones. Hence the statement of work for this type of engagement will not be light as it has to include details of the fixed price engagement and potential penalties for not delivering. Specific skills and experience are needed to formulate this type of statement of work.

Managing SLA and OLA defined engagements

An organisation may have Operating Level Agreements (OLAs) that define how the internal service providers will work together and provide services that are needed to deliver a defined Service Level Agreement (SLA) to the end client. Depending on which activities are offshored, there may be an OLA or an SLA that defines the service to be provided.

If the outsourcing vendor has committed to delivering services against this type of agreement and it forms part of the contractual statement of work then you must manage the vendor through that agreement. In this situation you would not expect to be paying for staff as per a T&M engagement but to be paying an agreed fixed cost for the outsourcing vendor to meet the criteria stated in the agreement.

It will be necessary to organise regular SLA or OLA reviews with the vendor. As part of the contractual obligation you should receive a regular report of how the engagement is meeting the criteria defined in the agreement according to the vendor. Despite this, you should always have an idea yourself on whether the agreement is being met. We have all heard stories of helpdesks that close tickets at the end of the day to make their statistics look better. This maybe little more than a myth but you need to be sure that when you see the figures that they mean the same thing to the vendor and the client.

Failure to meet the SLA or OLA criteria may incur penalties that were written into the statement of work. These could be cash penalties or senior escalations. Therefore this statement of work could be complicated and needs to be written by an expert and approved before it is issued.

Managing work throughput and predictability

When the vendor was selected you would have made a commitment on the total throughput of work the vendor should expect from the client. This commitment may have been no more than an indication or it may have been a contractual commitment to a minimum amount of work per year.

If your future work projections have changed in any way since the agreement, then it will be in your interests to communicate this to the vendor. The more predictable the engagement with the client can be, the lower the risks to the vendor, which should then equate to a lower cost for the client. For example, holding extra staff on the bench for a client costs money and this cost will find its way back to you one way or another.

Building relationships with the vendor

I advise you to make contact with the outsourcing vendor at different levels within their organisation in order to ensure the services are delivered to your satisfaction and that you can work around the issues that arise. Work your way up the vendor's organisation building relationships. If you get invited to meet the vendor's CEO then make sure you bring your list of issues with you as well as complementing him on the success of his organisation.

For a small engagement the vendor might well rely on one of the staff members he has provided you with being the day to day relationship manager. This has the benefit of the person being easily contacted and that he knows what is happening on the ground because he has real work to do himself. The disadvantage is that he might be distracted from doing the job he has been engaged for and he might spend too much time feeding back to his organisation what other opportunities there might be within your organisation.

A larger engagement will have a relationship manager appointed by the vendor. He will be a full time relationship manager even if he has other clients. Any issues or new requests must be raised to this person. Building a good working relationship with him will really help.

Remember that however much an outsourcing vendor tells you that he has a huge number of technical staff, there are never enough staff to go around all the clients. As a result of this, there is always an internal competition for the best staff. Therefore to get these staff you will need a relationship manager that can put a convincing case to his management.

If you work for a large global organisation then at an early stage it will be important to find out which other divisions of the global organisation use the same vendors as you. Business divisions are often strongly autonomous and they don't communicate who their vendors are. You can increase your leverage with the outsourcing vendor if you find that another business division is a big client and therefore your parent organisation is a bigger client than you thought.

If other parts of your group wide organisation use this same vendor then the next person to identify is the group relationship manager within the vendor's organisation. He may never have heard of your operating division or its requirements. You can increase your potential leverage by getting the group relationship manager to understand that failure in your engagements will look bad for all the engagements the vendor has with the group. He needs to believe that your organisation is joined up.

Negotiating once the contract has started

Negotiation with the vendor does not stop when the contract has been signed. When you manage the vendor right the way through to delivery then you will most likely also be negotiating with the outsourcing vendor until delivery. Once the contract has started then walking away is not a practical negotiation tactic, you need to resolve the perceived differences.

You need to keep in mind that the goal is for the IT service to be delivered. Therefore you may think that you are making good savings for the organisation by counting up the number of cash penalties that the outsourcing vendor has incurred but it may not help you to achieve the deliveries. Therefore when you negotiate with the vendor you need to always be thinking about how you can make the deliveries and perhaps how he can help you with other activities. An example of this is when you are unhappy with the quality of the staff on a project and you have waited a long time for a resolution, you can insist that the staff are replaced and that for making you wait their experts can come and help your team for a few days on another project where they are stuck.

The immediate power you have over the vendor is to not pay the bill at the end of the month. They know that you can do this if you end up in a dispute but it might cause all sorts of problems for them and for you. The ultimate power you have is to take your business elsewhere, this may lead not only to a loss of revenue but also to a reputational loss for the vendor.

IT services is a complex business. The vendor knows that you want to build a long term relationship and you don't want to change suppliers when you have a large number of engagements with that vendor and many are at a critical stage. So they may believe that you have little influence over them. If necessary you can demonstrate that you are not tied to this vendor alone by working with one or more of their competitors. So, for example, poor performance on one project may lead to you engaging their competitor for an upcoming project that they thought they were going to get for themselves. This sends a clear message.

On fixed price software deliveries and SLA defined engagements you will want to get an explanation from the vendor on how he is going to meet the required standards for the next month's review. This will be a more important use of the time available than discussing the cash penalties which are contractual anyway. If they don't have an improvement plan then you may need to look at alternative vendors for those activities.

Annual relationship appraisal

I suggest that there is a formal review of each vendor once per year. This is an opportunity to invite their senior management and to review the successes, failures, penalties and frustrations that occurred. It is also a good time to insist that certain improvements are made.

Benchmarking and repeating the RFP

When you have been in the relationship with the outsourcing vendor for at least one year then it will be time to compare what you are paying them with the market and to see if it is still competitive.

If you have been using the vendor for some years and the benchmarking is showing you that you could be getting better value for money elsewhere then it may be the right time to repeat the RFP process that you used to select the vendor in the first place. This does not mean that you would make a decision on cost alone and immediately move to the cheapest supplier. Rather, it is an opportunity for the outsourcing vendor to improve on his pricing or level of service in the face of documented competition. Although I would not rule out the possibility that the result of the RFP might really be to change vendors.

~~~

IT Offshoring Case Studies

Purpose of this section

This section uses lessons learned from real situations to present fictional case studies that illustrate the offshoring models and how transition is achieved. Any resemblance to actual transition projects in real organisations is purely coincidental.
A summary of the key facts is provided for each case.

The key facts include the following elements.
- Goal of the transformation
- Scope
- Transition type
- Offshore model
- Type of engagement
- Offshore location
- Billing model
- Cost savings achieved
- Final outcome

Case 1 - Front End Re-development

Goal	to preserve an application
Scope	a technology refresh
Transition type	knowledge transfer
Offshore model	managed service
Type of engagement	major offshore vendor
Offshore location	offshore centre
Billing model	time and materials
Cost savings	achieved
Final outcome	Success

The client had many business applications that were written in a particular supplier's technology suite. The technology supplier was still delivering new versions of the suite. The business applications were built using an old version of the technology which was no longer supported by the vendor, furthermore there were differences in how to use the technology. It was proving difficult to find staff that could maintain the applications. There was no backwards compatibility support between versions and no automated migration path. Any upgrade would require making code changes.

The client had decided that the applications either needed to be replaced or upgraded to the latest version of the vendor's technology. At the time there was not much budget available and the end users were not willing to work on a complete redesign. So the client decided a technology refresh would be a good solution. To keep it simple it was decided to not allow any functional improvements during the technology refresh.

An offshore solution provider had already been chosen by the client's senior management and therefore no further selection was undertaken. A meeting was called with the outsourcing vendor to ask them to demonstrate how they would undertake the work and whether they had the skills. During the meeting the vendor was able to name similar projects that they had completed for other clients and to show real CVs of staff that had the necessary skills.

Having agreed to start on a Time and Materials approach, the vendor sent two people to the client's onshore office to scope the activity. The two people interviewed the existing development staff and, once they were given access, they did their own analysis into the applications.

Following their trip onshore, the outsourcing vendor submitted a plan for the technology refresh of all 6 business applications. A cost projection was included based on the same time and materials approach. A fixed cost could not be given because the vendor identified too many areas where the onshore team was not able to give complete answers on some of the legacy parts of their applications.

At the time the vendor did not have a network connection to the client and therefore they were asked to work in the client's offshore centre.

The vendor soon demonstrated simple prototypes that proved that the migration was technically possible without a complete rewrite of the applications. Unfortunately, progress was slower than their initial plan. On investigation it was found that they didn't have a structured approach to the problem. The team was young and finding themselves away from their company processes and templates they were struggling. The client then had to spend time with them to define a structured approach.

Following this intervention from the client, deliveries started to arrive. Unfortunately the deliveries started to stack up and none of them were being accepted into production. This is because the client onshore team was not finding the time to test the applications. This required management intervention to resolve the blockage which then led to the discovery that there were many bugs. As a result of this the QA within the vendor team was changed and improved. Finally each application was tested in UAT by the client's key business users and the applications went into production.

The use of the managed service model was a success and the upgrade was managed autonomously with no day to day management from the client. The offshore team could work on their own, and if necessary they reverse engineered parts of the existing application to find out how it worked before implementing the same functionality in the new technology. There would have been no advantage in insisting to manage this from the client's onshore location.

Despite the time and cost overruns the technology upgrade was a success and was achieved for a much cheaper cost than if it was done by the client onshore.

Case 2 - Whole IT office transfer

Goal	reduce IT costs
Scope	full service
Transition type	full transition of products
Offshore model	managed service
Type of engagement	in-house
Offshore location	captive centre
Billing model	cost centre
Cost savings	achieved
Final outcome	success

An organisation was in desperate need to reduce costs. They were a very technology driven business and as a result had a large number of IT staff in multiple offices in high cost locations.

To achieve the desired savings it was decided by senior management to transfer a complete office of activity to a Captive Centre. By coincidence the organisation had purchased a technology company in a low cost location and was able to use this seed to grow an offshore centre. This was a huge transition task. It required the recruitment of large numbers of people in the offshore location and the execution of multiple full transition projects simultaneously. Unfortunately, because the cash situation was so tight, travel to the onshore location for training was not possible in most cases. Therefore it was necessary to devise ways to transfer knowledge by video conference, phone calls and email.

With the intention to disband and retrench all the onshore teams, the offshore team had no choice but to accept the products and activities as managed services. There would have been no possibility of using an extended team model. During the transition there was a gradual cut over of responsibility of each application to the offshore team until the complete office and all of its activities were transferred.

My personal opinion is that this transition to offshore was so ambitious that it would not even have started if it wasn't for the serious cost cutting instructed by the senior management. They had no other solution to cutting costs if they wanted to stay in business so they found a way to make it work.

Case 3 - Global Application Support Team Creation

Goal	follow the sun APS
Scope	APS
Transition type	knowledge transfer
Offshore model	follow the sun team
Type of engagement	in-house
Offshore location	captive centre
Billing model	cost centre
Cost savings	achieved
Final outcome	success

The organisation was expanding and doing more business in Asia. The analytics tools used by the business were supported in Europe and in the US but there were no staff covering the Asia time zone. The business sponsors didn't have the funds to create a new IT team in a high cost Asia location and so they asked for an alternative solution. The choice would have been between the existing teams working night shifts or the creation of an offshore team.

Members of the onshore team travelled to the offshore location and personally interviewed candidates for the recruitment of staff and the creation of the offshore team. When these candidates joined the Captive Centre they were systematically sent to the onshore location for knowledge transfer.

The knowledge transfer method was a combination of classroom training then job shadow and reverse job shadow. The offshore team made notes of their experiences which eventually became the training manuals that all the IT teams used across the world for these analytics tools. The onshore training sessions lasted 3 months for each person. When there were enough trained staff offshore then the support activities started. This was a progressive implementation, application by application aiming to minimise the risks. It was not really a cutover as no-one was yet providing this service for Asia.

Despite the slow ramp up and long training period onshore, the offshoring was cost effective. The team that was created offshore was highly knowledgeable and was able to take on more and more responsibilities beyond those originally planned.

Case 4 - Legacy Critical Banking Application Full Transition

Goal	cost savings
Scope	full service
Transition type	full transition
Offshore model	managed service
Type of engagement	in-house
Offshore location	captive centre
Billing model	cost centre
Cost savings	achieved
Final outcome	success

This particular application had been targeted for cost reduction many times in the past. As a result of this it already had an extended team offshore but their performance was disappointing and staff turnover was proving to be a problem. Encouragingly, the extended team did have good knowledge of some modules of the legacy application.

The users of this banking application were totally dependent on the application working throughout their business day and also for the overnight batch to work. So it was a near 24 hour support requirement.

The onshore team were very knowledgeable in the business of the users and had their own business analysts. This was needed because the functional improvements to the application requested by the users were significant. In fact the onshore team was also very experienced technically, with many having worked on this legacy application for more than 10 years.

One of the first steps was to recruit into the Captive Centre a senior manager who could be dedicated to this transition and then would manage the offshore team once complete. The next step was to produce a skills matrix for the onshore team, to calculate how many additional people would be needed offshore and to recruit them.

Once the offshore team was complete then they started to travel to the onshore location in small groups for the knowledge transfer. The method used was a mixture of classroom, job shadow and reverse job shadow. While on site the developers also started on maintenance activities under the guidance of the onshore team. Note that no single person in the offshore team was trained in every aspect of the application, but at the end of the transition the combined team had coverage of the whole application.

Each team member travelled to the onshore location twice during the transition and stayed for a minimum of one month. The direction and progress of each staff member's training was tracked on a skills and knowledge matrix throughout the transition and even continued afterwards during the operations phase. To overcome any issues with gaps in business knowledge, it was decided to send one of the offshore Business Analysts to the user's location on a 6 month rotation.

With the aim of retaining their good will, the staff of the onshore team were all offered equivalent roles in other teams before the transition started. This worked and all onshore team members remained professional and supported the transition until their team was disbanded. The transition was a success and congratulations was received from the user community as well as from IT management.

Note that despite this being a legacy application, enough talented people were found to work on the activity and this has continued over the last few years. It is also interesting to observe that what was an average extended team has become a very successful managed service team.

Despite the investment in 6 months of knowledge transfer, serious cost savings were achieved and continue to be achieved now that the team is completely offshore.

Case 5 - Recruitment Tool Outsourcing To Low Cost Provider

Goal	Save resources
Scope	development and maintenance
Transition type	full transition
Offshore model	managed service
Type of engagement	outsourcing
Offshore location	vendor's offices
Billing model	capped T&M
Cost savings	not achieved
Final outcome	success

The captive centre had developed a web based workflow application to manage the internal recruitment process. This was becoming a victim of its own success because it was critical to the recruitment process and it needed functional improvements but it was impossible to dedicate any Captive Centre staff to the development for more than a few weeks before they were needed on urgent "billable" projects for the parent company.

Therefore it was decided to outsource the development of the application to a vendor and to keep costs down. The chosen 3rd party vendor was a small boutique software house in a lower cost country.

The technical experts from the outsourcing vendor came to the offshore centre for 2 days to achieve the knowledge transfer. They worked with the main in-house developers to get a verbal understanding of how the application worked and what it was used for. Then they asked for an explanation of each of the outstanding functional improvements on the official list.

The application had been developed recently, with modern technologies and to a good standard. The vendor didn't produce new paper documents on how the application worked and therefore relied on the self-documentation of the code of the application and inserted comments. When the outsourcing vendor's technical experts returned to their office they trained a number of their own staff in how to develop on the application and the transition was complete.

The official list of outstanding functional requests was sent to the vendor and they started to deliver the enhancements. The list was regularly kept up to date and communicated. If one of the vendor's developers needed to know more then he would ask the user representative directly. Estimated dates were given for the delivery of the new features. This was enough information to manage the vendor and it was therefore a fully managed service by the vendor.

Note that in this case the outsourcing vendor didn't need a network connection to the offshore centre. The application used standard technologies and didn't need any proprietary technologies or in-house libraries for it to work. The vendor would send regular monthly emails with the latest source code which would be integrated, built and deployed in the Captive Centre. No major cost saving was achieved, but there was a big advantage in freeing up the in-house staff to work on parent company projects.

Case 6 - Workflow Tool Application Testing Offshoring

Goal	Offshore testing
Scope	application testing
Transition type	full, no staff reduction
Offshore model	managed service
Type of engagement	in-house
Offshore location	captive centre
Billing model	cost centre
Cost savings	achieved
Final outcome	success

An in-house developed workflow application was receiving functional improvements on a regular basis and it was necessary to ensure that existing functionality was not being compromised. The existing regression testing was being conducted by the on-shore business analyst and therefore it was reducing the time he could spend on new business analysis. Due to this compromise the official test scripts did not have a complete coverage of the application. So dedicated testing resources were needed and cost constraints dictated that these must be in the existing Captive Centre.

The application was being used by VIP salespeople within the organisation and they were intolerant of functional regression or new bugs being introduced.

Training was given to the offshore testing team remotely via screen sharing sessions and communication of existing documentation. No on-site visit was possible.

Once the offshore team had access to the application and the existing test scripts then they began to execute them on the current (already live) application. Any issues were discussed directly with the BA in the onshore location. This was a key part of the transition. At this stage the offshore team was ready to take over the activity themselves and to reproduce the exact same testing coverage for the next release of the workflow application.

The next stage was for the offshore team to increase the coverage of the existing tests. This was achieved either through their own initiative of what was missing or through reading the business analysis and release notes. The new tests were submitted to the BA for his review.

The testers were not managed directly from the onshore location. They would be informed of the next release, asked to test and communicated the new functionalities but that was all. Therefore this was a managed service. The application testing offshoring was a success and cost much less than if local resources had to be recruited onshore.

Sometime later there was a period of turnover in the testing team but they managed to recruit replacement staff and transfer the knowledge to them themselves and so the impact on the onshore team was minimal. Therefore the managed service model was working well.

Note that tests for major new functionality are still written and executed by the BA for the first release. Then the offshore team will integrate the BA tests into their scripts for the second and subsequent releases. This is their preferred method as it is the business analyst's commitment to ensure that the new functionality he defined works in the first delivery.

Case 7 - Build New Market Analysis and Transaction Processing Application

Goal	application replacement
Scope	develop a new application
Transition type	knowledge transfer
Offshore model	managed service
Type of engagement	in-house
Offshore location	captive centre
Billing model	cost centre
Cost savings	achieved
Final outcome	success

New businesses could not be added to an existing market analysis and transaction processing application and therefore it was decided to build a replacement application. Not enough budget was available to do it completely onshore and so it was decided to build the application in the Captive Centre as a managed service.

Training was given by the onshore team in how the existing application worked. This was achieved through one short onshore visit, exchange of documents and telephone meetings. The offshore team received a business analysis document stating the new functionality that would be needed. With this information they designed a new application that would include the old and new functionality.

The new application was built by the offshore team within the timescales proposed. Before the application could reach the system testing stage the onshore team changed and the new manager decided that he wanted much more input into what the team was doing. This was a major de-motivator for the offshore team as they had already achieved so much on their own.

Despite this, the new manager did add value by using his onshore presence to progress issues with other teams onshore and to get answers to integration questions. As a result of their combined efforts the application was successfully delivered into production.

Case 8 - Offshore IT Development Tools

Goal	cost reduction
Scope	support and enterprise integration
Transition type	full transition
Offshore model	managed service
Type of engagement	in-house
Offshore location	captive centre
Billing model	cost centre
Cost savings	not achieved
Final outcome	failure

A global organisation had a centralised team in a high cost location that supported all the open source IT development tools used by their IT developers across the world. These development tools included source code repositories and source code analysis applications. Because these applications were open source there was no external third party support available and no vendor that would ultimately accept responsibility for any problems. Ideally the team should have been focussed only on the production support of these applications but in practice these applications were not enterprise ready and therefore they were having to build these tools from their source code and to integrate them into the organisation's IT infrastructure. This integration work was needed every time that there was a new version of one of the tools.

This team had come under the cost saving spotlight some years before and as a result it had one team member already offshore in the organisation's Captive Centre. The remaining team members were external contractors in the high cost location. Each of them were experts in these open source development tools, they had worked with them for years at different corporations. The team came under that same spotlight again when a Discovery exercise was conducted and the head of IT noticed that there was a non-business facing team in the high cost location that didn't have many people offshore and saw this as an opportunity to save costs.

The development support team reported into the Application Production Support (APS) manager. When he was informed by the IT Efficiency Task Force that his team was under review, he reminded everyone what the situation with these tools was like 3 years previously. He explained that some 3000 developers were dependent on these tools working properly, that the source code for all the critical applications was managed by these tools and that the organisation could not afford to put these tools at risk again. Without the source code the critical systems of the organisation could not be built or maintained. So the matter was escalated to senior IT management who promptly replied that these were only development tools and therefore there was nothing to stop them being offshored.

Understanding that some form of further offshoring was inevitable, the APS manager started looking at the different offshoring options. Before he could reach a conclusion the IT Efficiency Task Force contacted him again and said that they had been given instructions to present two offshoring scenarios for the IT Development Tools team to senior management the very next day, one low risk scenario and one "stretch" scenario that would achieve maximum cost savings but with higher risk. The APS manager documented the two scenarios and used the standard offshoring template to illustrate the transition plan and to calculate the total savings. The IT Efficiency Task Force received both scenarios but, for reasons known only to them, they presented the "stretch" scenario to senior IT management and didn't mention the lower risk scenario. As a result of this the high risk scenario was approved and the APS manager was told to start the project. The APS manager was furious that he had been tricked in this way. He protested and explained again what was at stake but no-one was listening.

The APS manager was someone who believed in sharing information with his team and he did not like keeping management secrets. So once it was clear to him that he had to implement the "stretch" offshoring plan then he announced to the IT Development Tools team that there were going to be some changes and he explained the offshoring plan in the most neutral way he could. The team didn't take it very well and they offered their predictions that within one year of offshoring that there would be a production problem that could not be resolved. Within two weeks of this meeting one of the team members gave notice that he would be leaving for another opportunity. Publically he didn't say that his move was prompted by the offshoring but everyone suspected it was.

Two months later the transition project had not really progressed. The recruitment of staff in the Captive Centre was on the critical path but after two months no candidates had been accepted. On investigation it was found that the APS manager had insisted that no staff should be recruited until he had personally approved them. The job specification for the offshore team members was exactly the same one that was used in the onshore location and it contained specific references to years of experience which could never have been achieved offshore and probably were not necessary either. It looked as though the team and their manager were finding ways to slow the offshoring down in the hope that it would be eventually abandoned.

The IT Efficiency Task Force had noticed that no progress was being reported for this transition project and so they escalated it to their management. This resulted in a clear message being sent to the APS manager that he was personally responsible for offshoring this team and meeting his cost targets within the budget year. No excuses would be accepted.

After some deliberation, the APS manager re-wrote his job specifications with the help of the Captive Centre management and as a result candidates started to be identified. Unfortunately, by this time 2 more members of the onshore team had handed in their notice bringing the total number of departures to 3, out of a total team size of 6 people. Everyone knew that if the transition didn't start soon then there would be no knowledge left onshore to achieve the knowledge transfer and then the transition offshore couldn't possibly happen.

Within a couple of months new employees were arriving in the Captive Centre for the IT Development Tools team. To speed the process up the Captive Centre added 2 new graduates to the team knowing that this would be two less people to recruit. Eventually the offshore team was starting to take shape. The one experienced offshore team member started training the new recruits on how to support the tools. This sounded good in the weekly offshore transition meetings until the APS manager dropped a bombshell. The one team member offshore had only ever supported the applications, he had never built the applications from source code or integrated them with the rest of the IT infrastructure. Therefore the new recruits were learning simple support tasks, but they would not be in a position to replace the onshore team. The APS manager suggested that all the new recruits should come to the onshore location for training while there was still a team left to train them.

The IT Efficiency Task Force rejected the request for the whole team to travel. They said that the APS manager had written his own offshore transition project, it was his figures that were accepted by senior management and now he had to deliver exactly those cost savings. Furthermore, any failure to deliver these cost savings for the IT Development Tools project would require a balancing reduction somewhere else. The APS manager felt betrayed by this. His own figures were now being used against him. He took a practical approach and authorised the travel for only two offshore team members and accepted that they would have to train the other team members themselves as soon as they returned to the offshore location.

At the next weekly offshore transition meeting, the team leader of the onshore IT Development Tools team announced that he would be leaving in 2 months' time, this was 6 months earlier than planned. This left 2 months to train the team as much as possible. Every effort was made to train the offshore staff. In addition to the onshore training there was remote training by screen sharing and even small integration projects that were executed under the supervision of the onshore team. At the end of the two months the offshore team was handling most of the work including all of the support requests during their working hours. This was as good an outcome as could have been achieved given the circumstances and it was only achieved thanks to the remaining good-will onshore and the keenness and hard work of the offshore team. At the end of this period the onshore team leader left as per his announcement. He was quickly followed by the rest of his team who also left earlier than planned.

The IT Development Tools area continued to function well offshore for a further 8 months. Then the global developer community started to raise concerns that their development was being affected by the slowness of the development tools. Apparently the development tools had been gradually slowing down and the new offshore support team was not aware of this. This continued for a few more months, during which time the speed was becoming noticeably slower to everyone. The offshore team felt under pressure to resolve the situation but they couldn't find the cause, there was no-one to help them, and so the problem continued.

Very soon afterwards the developers lost confidence in the offshore team and escalated their issues to senior management. Three months later, and without any consultation, the senior IT management announced that a new set of IT Development Tools (from a third party vendor) would be replacing the open source tools and that a new team onshore would replace the offshore support team and there would be a short period of migration to the new tools. Once the migration was complete, the offshore team was disbanded and although the staff were offered other roles they all chose to leave the Captive Centre as a result of the experience that they had had.

In conclusion the offshore transition didn't achieve the long term cost savings that had been targeted. For a full 8 months it looked as though the offshore transition had been a success. Unfortunately the knowledge transfer had not been in enough depth to allow the new staff to fully maintain the systems and no-one was kept onshore to mitigate this risk. Internal politics and an old fashioned "command and control" attitude from senior management also had a part to play in why a transition that was identified as being risky was allowed to go ahead in this way.

Case 9 - Offshore Client Data Management

Goal	cost reduction
Scope	data operations and administration
Transition type	extended team
Offshore model	extended team
Type of engagement	in-house
Offshore location	captive centre
Billing model	cost centre
Cost savings	achieved
Final outcome	success

A sales team had a central application in which they would store specific information on current clients and potential clients for event management purposes. This information was supplementary to the information that could be found in the company's CRM. Also it was integrated with some other tools that made it difficult to replace. There was a team of people within the sales department whose job it was to maintain the data in the system. As the organisation had grown so had the client data administration team. It was at the point where there were easily enough people to split the team with the Captive Centre, create an extended team and reduce costs.

The Client Data Manager was aware that this transfer of activity would be controversial and it could have legal implications. Therefore before starting the transition he invited a representative from the company's legal department and a representative from the company's compliance department to a meeting where he outlined his plans and asked for their advice. The legal representative raised the very real concern that the offshoring could not take place unless each client expressly authorised that its data could be stored offshore. In addition to this the compliance representative said that the organisation would need to apply to the government regulator before this type of offshoring could be undertaken.

Following this rather depressing meeting the Client Data Manager came to speak to the IT Offshore Programme Manager to see if he could help. The programme manager was not convinced that what had been proposed was the only way forward and he believed that these issues must already have been resolved before for an IT offshore project. So he did some research and then invited himself to their next meeting.

In the meeting the IT Offshore Programme Manager explained how offshoring was working for the existing IT teams. He stated the difference between offshoring to a Captive Centre and outsourcing to a third party. He said that security was very tight in the Captive Centre (more so than in the onshore locations) and he presented the meeting participants with a detailed security review that had recently been conducted by an independent third party consultancy giving the Captive a strong security rating. In the review document he pointed out that the existing offshore operations activities did not include local data storage of any kind, there were no local files or local databases. The operations users were accessing central application servers through Citrix, they couldn't print the information on their screens and all USB ports had been disabled on their PCs so no information could be taken away. This was not what the compliance and legal representatives had understood from the last meeting. Given this new information, they agreed to go away and do their own research before revising their earlier pronouncements.

At the next meeting the legal department representative declared that there was no legal risk and the feasibility discussion need only continue with the compliance representative. Since the last meeting the compliance representative had been doing his own research as promised. He had reached the conclusion that the whole Captive Centre should be making a statement to the local regulator explaining what it was doing, but that this was not a prerequisite for starting the offshoring. Therefore it would be enough to start writing the documents to make the announcement to the regulator in parallel with continuing the offshore transitions to the Captive Centre. This meeting was closed on a very positive note with the Client Data Manager knowing that these particular problems that could have blocked his offshore project completely were now resolved.

Following further study of the feasibility of the offshore project, the Client Data Manager organised an offshoring kick-off steering committee. He invited the same two legal and compliance representatives to the steering committee and made sure that they were on record in the meeting as stating that they had no objections to the offshoring of the client data management activity.

The offshore transition itself was a success. The onshore team was reduced in size and the offshore team proved to be just as productive as the onshore team. Within 12 months the targeted cost savings had been achieved and the offshoring was declared a success.

Case 10 - Offshore Accounts Payable Activity

Here follows a BPO transition case study for the Accounts Payable function within a company. The purpose of including this is to illustrate how the same principles used for IT transition are used to achieve the transition of a (non-IT) financial operations activity.

Goal	cost reduction
Scope	accounts payable operations
Transition type	full transition
Offshore model	managed service
Type of engagement	in-house
Offshore location	captive centre
Billing model	profit centre
Cost savings	achieved
Final outcome	success

The first step was for the BPO analysts to visit the client site to understand exactly how they did accounts payable. They needed to know what tools were used, what documents were used, what processes were being followed, the current volumes and what reports were being created.

It was then necessary to advise on the changes needed to be made in order for the processes to be offshored. In this case a recommendation was made that all paper processes would be replaced by electronic processes. Therefore all paper invoices coming from the suppliers would be scanned and stored. From that point on the team would only work on the scanned images in the document management system and never use the paper documents except in the case of disputes.

The second part of the recommendation was to implement a workflow system to manage the flow of the electronic documents from receipt of invoice to payment. Note that the approach would be classified as "lift and shift" because the offshore team were solely responsible for implementing the recommendations.

With the understanding reached with the onshore management that the recommendations would need to be accepted if offshoring was to take place, the next step was to take the process that was documented during the visit onshore and redesign it so that it worked with the new electronic tools. Once complete it was possible to calculate the cost of implementation, the cost of transition, how many people would be needed in the offshore team and then to estimate the ongoing yearly operational cost. These results were fed into the team's business case document template and submitted to the onshore management for approval.

The Captive Centre was a profit centre. This allowed the team to quote a guaranteed fixed price for the yearly operational cost of the accounts payable service. However, the transition project itself was recharged as time and materials as it was the first one and there was a risk that the onshore team would delay the transition if they were not comfortable.

Following the approval from the onshore management, then the next stage was to organise a knowledge transfer from the onshore team. This was achieved with a combination of class room sessions, job shadow and reverse job shadow. The business knowledge of what to do with the invoices would still be needed even though the offshore processes were different due to the use of the electronic tools. Only the senior members of the offshore team travelled to the onshore location for the knowledge transfer. When the senior members returned then they shared their information with the remaining staff and thus trained them. Hence there was a cost saving achieved compared to sending the whole team to the onshore location.

While onshore, the senior members of the offshore team made sure that the small team of people who would scan and categorise the incoming invoices had been fully trained in the new processes. These would be the only people to remain onshore in this transition. It was unavoidable because the paper documents had to be physically scanned by a person at their point of origin and without delay.

With the tools implemented and the staff trained, the cutover from the onshore team and their semi-manual process to the offshore team and their electronic process was then ready to begin. To reduce the transition risk, the invoices were split into different categories. This allowed the offshore team to start their activity with one low volume category. Once the first category was being successfully processed offshore then gradually more categories were added until all the invoices were being processed offshore and nothing was left onshore.

The onshore team continued to help the offshore team with any queries for a few weeks following the transition, after which the onshore team was no longer needed. The onshore team were then redeployed to other departments.

Within a year the offshore team identified some major improvements to the processes and was therefore able to reduce the yearly costs. Some of the cost savings were shared with the onshore client, thus reducing their yearly invoices. The remainder of the cost savings were retained as profit by the Captive Centre for re-investment into new activities. Note that this was only possible because the Captive Centre had been created around the principles of the profit centre model.

The transition was a complete success and it led to other countries in the group offshoring their accounts payable activity to similar teams under the same offshore BPO manager.

###

Thank-you for reading my book. If you enjoyed it and you found it useful, then please take a moment to leave me a review for this book on your retailer's website.

Thanks!
Clive Verrall

Glossary

Agile: In this context Agile is used as an abbreviation for Agile Software Development Methods which includes Kanban, Scrum and Extreme Programming.

Bench: A pool of people who are intentionally not assigned to client activities so that they can be made available immediately for any new activities.

Body Shopping: When an outsourcing vendor supplies people to the client without any other value added services.

BOT: Build Operate and Transfer. An outsourcing vendor creates an ODC for a client with the contractual commitment to transfer ownership to the client within a specified schedule.

BPO: Business Process Offshoring. Analysis and transition of non-IT business activities from onshore to offshore.

Captive: Abbreviation of Captive Centre.

Captive Centre: An ODC built by the parent organisation for its own internal activities and not to provide services to the external market.

Centre of excellence: Grouping of experts for a particular subject into a centralised team that can provide consultancy to other teams therefore liberating them from needing their own experts.

CMMi: Capability Maturity Model Integration. A process improvement and appraisal global standard. Ratings are from 1 to 5; where 5 is the highest level of process maturity.

Cost centre captive: A captive that is obliged to charge its parent company the exact cost incurred in supplying its services.

Delivery Centre: The place where IT work takes place. This could be a Captive Centre or a Vendor ODC.

Extended team: A team in two locations under the same onshore management to achieve the same objectives.

Fix and shift: Tasking the onshore team to make improvements before offshoring.

Follow the sun: Methodology to provide 24 hour services by having staff in three locations across the world.

Full service offshoring: In the IT world this is the offshoring of development, maintenance, testing and support for the same application.

Full transition: Transfer of a complete activity offshore such that no staff or activity are left onshore.

GIC: A Global Insourcing Centre is a Captive Centre that also conducts insourcing activities where outsourced activities are transitioned back to the client's premises.

HR: Human Resources is the department within a company that takes care of the staff including recruitment and setting salary guidelines.

Internal ODC: See Captive Centre.

KPI: Key Process Indicators are statistical measures of an activity.

KT: The process of Knowledge Transfer is to pass information from an established team to a new recruit or new team so that they can then be productive.

Lift and shift: Transition of activities offshore exactly as they are with the intention to do any improvements offshore.

Managed service: Self-managed team of people that are measured on their deliveries.

MSA: A Master Services Agreement is a contract containing the terms and conditions that will be referenced for each engagement with the service supplier.

Near shore: Similar to offshoring but only using countries that are nearby, e.g. in the same continent.

ODC: Offshore Delivery Centre. The premises, management staff and services needed to offshore activities.

Offshore: Located in a lower cost country.

Offshore centre: Could be a vendor ODC or Captive Centre depending on the context.

Offshore model: Pattern used to achieve work offshore, typically defines the location of staff and their level of autonomy.

Offshore partner: An outsourcing vendor with whom there is a long term relationship.

OLA: Operating Level Agreement is a support services agreement typically between internal providers on what they need to achieve in order to collectively deliver a service to their end users.

Onshore: The home location, typically in a high cost developed country.

Outsourcing: Transfer of an activity from one organisation to a 3rd party offshore service provider.

Outsourcing vendor: A 3rd party offshore service provider that specialises in transition activities offshore and delivering those activities from offshore.

Over recruitment: Recruiting staff whose skills, experience or ambition is greatly in excess of that needed for the role.

Product oriented offshoring: Organising offshore teams around products and thus creating a portfolio of related product teams.

Profit Centre Captive: A captive centre that can choose how much to charge its parent company for the services that it supplies.

Risk Register: Complete list of all the key risks for a project with their likelihood of occurring and the impact if they do occur.

Shared Utilities: The homogenisation of disparate applications and teams that serve the same core purpose in to one application and one global team. Typically involves providing the target service from offshore.

SLA: A Service Level Agreement defines what targets need to be achieved based on rules and specific criteria in order to deliver a defined service to the end users.

SSC: A Shared Service Centre can be thought of as a Captive Centre which has some services that span multiple business lines of the parent company and are therefore shared.

Staff Augmentation: See Body Shopping.

Statement of work (SOW): Contract for a particular service or delivery that refers to the terms and conditions agreed in the MSA.

Sunset: Management of IT applications that are at the end of their lives.

Synergies: Efficiencies that can be gained in terms of time, money or resources.

T&M: Time and materials is a billing model where costs are allocated based on the number of man days spent and the cost of any materials used.

Technology oriented offshoring: Organising offshore teams around the technologies that they use and thus creating a portfolio of teams that use the same technologies.

Transformation synergies: Efficiencies achieved as part of a large business transformation.

Vendor ODC: A secure area where the outsourcing vendor does work for one client.

WOOS: For Wholly Owned Operating Subsidiary see Captive Centre.

~~~

About the Author

Clive Verrall has been involved in IT offshoring since 1998. He has been a client for many outsourcing companies as well as building and managing the primary offshoring centre for a global financial services group over a period of 7 years, of which more than 5 years were spent living in India. During his time at the offshoring centre he managed the early pilot projects with less than 10 people, then grew the centre to more than 700 people and made yearly multi-million dollar savings for the parent company. Although the centre initially focussed on IT offshoring it expanded to include back office business operations and front office support functions.

Early in his career the author has worked in IT for software houses in the UK and since then he has completed 20 years in financial services IT and is more recently a freelance consultant.

During his offshoring career the author is grateful to have had the opportunity to be invited to see so many organisations' offshore activities. These insights took place either as a potential client, as an exchange of information between professionals or to provide management consultancy.

These activities have given him insight and experience of offshoring in Asia, Europe (near shore), North Africa, South America and North America (near shoring for the US).

The author can be contacted using the form:
https://www.cliveverrall.com/contact

Find out more about the author and his current book projects at https://www.cliveverrall.com/books

~~~

Acknowledgements

The author would like to express his gratitude to the following people for spending their time reviewing the book and providing comprehensive feedback. Without their good will, patience and hard work this book would not be as it is today.

Adam Wolszczak, Poland.

Brillian SK, India.

Manish Ahuja, India.

Abhishek Verma, United Arab Emirates.

Radek Sawa, Poland.

Wendy Agnes Bijlsma, United Kingdom.

Tracy Pascoe, Australia.

Amit Thawani, Australia.

~~~

Other books by this author

Inside Information Technology at a Top Tier Investment Bank
By Clive Verrall

What do you need to know to become successful in investment banking IT? How does investment banking IT work, what are the essential concepts and the critical IT systems? This book is aimed at anyone in IT who wants to increase their understanding of the rewarding world of investment banking IT. It will be of benefit both to people who know very little about investment banking and want a complete introduction to gain entry and it will also be useful to those who already have experience and want to get a robust understanding of the subject to accelerate their career.

Investment banking is a complicated collection of subjects. It is no surprise that the IT systems built for investment banking can also be complicated and are often implemented only by people who have an in-depth understanding of a particular niche of the investment banking business for which the system is needed. This in-depth knowledge takes years to accumulate and as a result IT staff with that knowledge are hard to find and are well paid. This makes it difficult for new comers to break into this large and still growing IT area or even to switch domains within a bank once they have already started. In this book I will share my experiences gained over more than 20 years to fast track the reader's career.

Throughout the book investment banking activities are explained in the context of what their demands on the IT department are. For each activity area this includes looking at system diversity, IT team sizes, IT process maturity, technologies used, key IT roles and whether advanced mathematical skills are needed.

Find out more about this book and other books by this author at https://www.cliveverrall.com/books

~~~

www.ingramcontent.com/pod-product-compliance
Lightning Source LLC
Chambersburg PA
CBHW031626210526
45464CB00004B/1762